EMPATH AND PSYCHIC ABILITIES

A Survival Guide for Highly Sensitive People.
Guided Meditations to Open Your Third Eye,
Expand Mind Power, Develop Intuition,
Telepathy, and Clairvoyance

by

MINDFULNESS LODGE

with

May Rowland and Sai Chakra Barti

Text Copyright © [MINDFULNESS LODGE]

Legal & Disclaimer

Part I

ENHANCE YOUR PSYCHIC ABILITIES

You are standing next to your window, watching the world go by. You can see people walking down the street, old and young alike, each minding their own business. But you are sure of one thing – you're scared of being one of those people. If it were possible, you would rather spend the entire day in your apartment. In your experience, being around people can be extremely overwhelming because you seem to go through a roller coaster of emotions.

Each moment you spend out there, you are unsure of what emotion you will feel next. Frustration, excitement, grief, anxiety, joy, angst, annoyance, you name it. Thanks to your introspective mind, you have found out that you only feel these emotions when you are surrounded by people. And it's precisely why you have developed a tendency of running away from them every time you get overwhelmed.

There must be a deep cry from the depths of your soul; what am I?

You are an empath.

You have the special gift of soaking up the energies floating around you and perceiving them as though they were your own. Being an empath is a gift – not a curse. So, it is high time you learned more about your capabilities.

CHAPTER 1: HOW TO DEVELOP YOUR PSYCHIC ABILITIES

Although you have psychic potential, you still have to train yourself so that your skills may become finely tuned.

THE FOLLOWING ARE SOME TIPS TO HELP YOU ENHANCE YOUR PSYCHIC ABILITIES

MEDITATE EVERYDAY

Meditation allows you to raise your vibration. The spirit energy vibrates at a high frequency. Through meditation, you can heighten your mental and spiritual powers and become capable of performing even greater psychic acts. Meditation is not a resource-intensive activity. You can pull it off almost anywhere. You just require a serene environment and some free time.

COMMUNICATE WITH YOUR SPIRIT GUIDE

Your spirit guide is basically an entity that protects you. They also enlighten you and make you insightful. When you call on their support, you will increase your chances of achieving what you desire. Have a sacred place in which you meet your spirit guide.

USE PSYCHOMETRY

Psychometry is the practice of decoding the energies of an object. If you can become skilled in this discipline, you will receive a tremendous boost to your psychic abilities. Acquire an object that has sentimental value – e.g., a wedding band – and try to envision the energies of the owner.

FLOWER VISUALIZATION

To have strong psychic abilities, you have to improve your mind's eye. You can achieve this through flower visualization. The exercise entails picking up a few flowers and holding them in front of you.

Now close your eyes and start envisioning each of them separately.

RANDOM VISUALIZATION

When you are done using the flower to strengthen your mind's eye, you may now explore some randomness. Just close your eyes and lie on your back in a serene environment and invite your spirit guides to show you many great wonders of the universe. Your spirit guides should show you magnificent images and videos.

TAKE A WALK-IN NATURE

Psychics feel a tremendous connection with nature. You could take a stroll in a nature park while practicing mindful meditation. Take occasional stops by sweet-smelling flowers and savor their beauty. Lose yourself to the beauty of nature.

ELIMINATE NEGATIVITY

You cannot tap into your psychic powers if you harbor tons of negativity. Eliminate your negativity by heightening your self-awareness and being more forgiving to yourself. You also have to take the necessary steps to right the wrongs you have done. Once you're free of negativity, you're in the right headspace to employ your psychic powers.

BELIEVE IN YOURSELF

You cannot become a skilled clairvoyant unless you have tremendous belief in yourself. One of the ways of increasing your self-belief is through reading about those before you who have succeeded.

Find books written by successful clairvoyants and read about them so that you can become familiar with their stories. Learn their tricks. The more you study about successful clairvoyants, the higher your odds of becoming successful yourself.

REST

Quality rest is absolutely necessary. The more you rest, the more energy you have to channel into your psychic activities. One of the best ways to ensure quality rest is by getting enough sleep. You should get at least six hours of sleep every night. This will ensure that your mind is well rested and you're in top physical condition. Having enough rest is crucial for the development of your clairvoyant skills.

TRY TO READ OTHER PEOPLE'S THOUGHTS

This is a perfect way of strengthening your clairvoyant abilities. When you encounter someone, just gaze into their eyes and try to imagine what they are thinking about. If you can accurately read people's minds, then you can rest assured that your psychic abilities are very well developed.

KEEP TRACK OF YOUR DREAMS

People with psychic abilities tend to dream a lot. After each dream, ensure you have noted it down on a journal. This will help you keep track of the dreams that came true. When you realize that your dreams are starting to become true, it indicates that your clairvoyant abilities are getting fine-tuned.

IMPROVE YOUR REMOTE-VIEWING CAPABILITY

Remote viewing is the ability to view a place or an event through your mind's eye without you being physically present. To improve your ability of remote viewing, you have to make good use of your imagination. Start with viewing places near you, and when you get them right, you can move on to far-flung places and objects.

OVERCOME YOUR FEARS

If you have any fear in your mind, you will not achieve your full potential as a clairvoyant. You have to eliminate the fear to be able to channel all your mental energies in your psychic activities. The first step toward eliminating fear is to increase your knowledge. The more you know about a situation, the less ignorant you are and the more power and courage you acquire.

RESOLVE YOUR DIFFERENCES WITH THOSE AROUND YOU

If you have problems with other people, ensure that you resolve them. You cannot achieve your full clairvoyant potential when you are not at peace with yourself or other people. Cast away the burden of bitterness and resolve your differences with those around you. This way, your mind is in a position to channel its energies into psychic activities.

PRACTICE SEEING AURAS

This is another great exercise for improving your psychic abilities. Have your friend stand next to a plain-colored wall. Then, look at them using your third eye. Notice if you get to see their auric field. If they have a high vibration, their aura will appear bright.

ASK A FRIEND TO CALL YOU

Contact your friend telepathically and ask them to give you a call. The more mental energy you invest in this activity, the more likely your friend will call you. If an empath developed their psychic potential, they could end up becoming so skilled that a career along that line would be in order.

CHAPTER 2: INTUITION

An intuitive empath has a profound capacity of intuiting the thoughts and actions of people. This ability has been with them ever since they were small. An intuitive empath is a special kind of empath, and the following traits are distinct to them:

VIVID DREAMS

An intuitive empath experiences vivid dream. These dreams are never lost on an empath. This capability of theirs started when they were small kids and has stuck with them into adulthood. Intuitive empaths are very much in love with the dream world and can't seem to wait for the night so that they can jump into another dream.

Considering that dreams bypass the ego, they are usually very powerful mediums of providing intuitive information. Dreams bring about guidance on matters of spirituality and healing, as well as overcoming terrible emotions. Dream elements may be symbolic too. However, an intuitive empath is equipped to decode the hidden meaning of every character that appears in their dreams. The dream of an empath is more often than not message laden.

Maybe it's a revelation or a healing message. Intuitive empaths utilize these dreams in providing solutions for what ails them or the people that they care about. Some intuitive empaths have spirit guides whom they talk to within the dream world. The spirit guide can take the shape of an animal, person, angel, or even voice, but their presence is unmistakable. Spirit guides normally give you the wisdom of overcoming your life challenges, actualizing your goals, and living more creatively and peaceably. Spirit guides have no malicious intent and are actually interested in improving the life of the intuitive empath along with their friends. During dreams, an intuitive empath has the capability of moving from the present world and touring through the dream-verse. This is called an out-of-body experience. It is surreal.

An empath who is used to this kind of experience can find themselves missing sleeping, as they cannot wait to go on another trip into the worlds beyond our thin veil of reality. The dream-history of intuitive empaths is extensive and to ensure that none of that is lost, you have to record it. When you wake up, write down the details of your dream in a journal. Then meditate on the meaning of those dreams during the rest of the day. Get into the habit of asking yourself significant questions before you go to bed. This way, you will encourage your spirit guides to give you an answer through a dream.

MYSTIC CAPABILITIES

Another sure sign of an intuitive empath is their mystic powers. An intuitive empath is the type of person to take a casual glance at someone and read their minds like a textbook. They know what your hidden thoughts are, what you are about to do, and what you truly think about various things. An intuitive empath is the sort of person that will think to themselves, "My mom has gone two days without speaking to me," and just as they contemplate that absurdity, their phone will start buzzing and guess who's calling? Momma! An intuitive empath is the sort of person who will be sitting around and suddenly think, "My child is sick," and then they will learn later that their child is sick.

An intuitive empath faces the challenge of detecting whether a certain thought that they have is independent or a projection of their emotions and struggles. Chances of a thought being accurate are high when that thought appears independently, as opposed to it being an extension of an intuitive empath's emotional state. It is absolutely necessary for an intuitive empath to develop a profound sense of self-awareness. Information received when you're in a neutral or compassionate state is far more accurate than messages received when you are emotionally charged. However, if an intuitive empath has a profound understanding of self, they will hardly project their fears, worries, or insecurities onto other people.

As an intuitive empath, it is absolutely necessary for you to stay grounded. The vibrations you pick up off of other people shouldn't complicate your life. On the contrary, they should deepen your compassion and understanding for others. The ability to read into people's hidden thoughts is rare. At the back of your mind, you should know that you're extremely fortunate.

CONNECTED TO MOTHER EARTH

Intuitive empaths are very much connected to mother earth. They can perceive various natural bodies – sensually and energetically. If it's the thunder, they can perceive its power rattling through their body, and if it's the moon, they can perceive its beauty welling up inside them. An intuitive empath seems to be attuned to the energy status of the earth. They are happy when mother earth is well taken care of, and sad when mother earth acts with fury. If an intuitive empath lives near the ocean and the waters are calm, the empath will feel nourished and happy. However, if the waters become violent, the initial happiness escapes them, and in its place, comes depression.

The intuitive empath is such unicorn, for they are happy when the earth is in great condition, and sad when the earth suffers any harm. For this reason, the empath must take an active role in ensuring that the earth is well taken care of. The intuitive empath must also spend time in the natural world to experience the state of oneness.

FOREKNOWLEDGE OF EVENTS

If you're an intuitive empath, you find yourself often telling people, "Didn't I tell you?" This is because you seem to have prior knowledge of things. Either you get visions about the future when you're awake, or you dream about future events, but in both cases, the visions come to pass. This ability is not restricted to your life alone. You may very well predict the future events of other people's lives. You can see what their relationships, careers, and other statuses will be like. Being an intuitive empath is an immense gift that one should be proud of and take full advantage of to have a fulfilling life.

INTUITION PITFALLS

People want to have a smooth and easy transition between realms. Some find the transition to be difficult and end up feeling disoriented and want to remedy this. An easy transition doesn't just come about, it requires effort. It requires an excellent balance. Vibrations and frequencies are the most important parts of every experience. Higher vibrations are the result of the range of the frequency. If you have higher vibrations, that's probably what is causing the rough transition. Increasing your intuition will help you to sense and see metaphysical movements that take place during transitions. With an open third eye, you will be able to sense these things more precisely. You will also be able to break down the frequencies and vibrations. Here are some ways to avoid pitfalls.

LISTEN TO YOURSELF

People frequently ignore when their body is trying to tell them something. They are working to open and work with their third eye, but they neglect the rest of their body. It is scientifically proven that there are neurotransmitters in the stomach, so your gut has the ability to tell you something. It's important not to ignore these gut feelings. When you begin your third eye work, tell yourself and set the intention that you will pay attention to mind and your gut. It's important to trust your body.

KEEP TRACK OF DREAM

Our dreams aren't just there to give your mind something to do while you sleep. Your dreams are messages from your subconscious, so it's important to not ignore them. Start to keep a dream journal. Keep track of what your dreams are telling you and start to look for similarities. These similarities could be something important that your mind is trying to tell you.

VISIT A NATURAL HABITAT

As humans, we pretty much live in a concrete jungle. Many of us don't socialize with nature the way we need to, and our bodies need that. Everybody needs nature, but a person with an awakened third eye craves the touch of nature. Take time out of your day just to walk outside and put your bare feet on the ground. Go hiking once a month or you can even cuddle with a pet. The touch of an animal helps to recharge you just like nature, and many times your pet can sense it. It also gives your mind a chance to relax from all the distractions of electronics in your life.

GET REPETITIVE

A great way to relax your mind and open your intuition and third eye is to take up a repetitive physical action. This could mean running, cooking, dancing, playing a musical instrument, or painting. The list of the things you could choose to do is endless. These types of activities help calm your mind and open your abilities of intuition.

RELEASE RESISTANCE

Don't try to fight the feelings you get. Embrace these new-found feelings. They are there to help you not hurt you. Once you have learned how to embrace these new feelings, instead of resisting them, then you will be able to comfortably work with your third eye. Resistance is probably your biggest adversary when working with your third eye.

CHAPTER 3: TELEPATHY

Have you ever watched a movie where two people communicate just with their minds or where someone reads another person's thoughts to gain information?

HAVE YOU EVER WISHED YOU COULD DO THAT?

Telepathy (from the Greek "tele" meaning "far away" and "patheia" meaning "to be affected by") is communication between minds – but like all aspects of psychic ability, it's not exactly how it's depicted in the movies. However, it is possible to practice telepathy in real life; it's just subtler. You may have even done so without meaning to, for example, if you've ever been thinking about someone or really wishing to hear from someone, and soon after they call or text out of nowhere with no previous planning.

This is a form of telepathic communication. The two of your minds were communicating without knowing it, causing the person who called you to make the decision to call – or maybe their decision to call is what brought them into your mind and got you thinking about them. It's no coincidence when things like this happen. There are always psychic channels at work in situations such as these, and like psychic premonitions, everyone has the ability to use telepathy; it's just an area in our mind that needs to be exercised but that most of us ignore or don't believe in due to how we were raised, the society or religion we were brought up in, etc. Those that have been brought up encouraged to expand the mind and pursue psychic and telepathic abilities will have an easier time with this, but that doesn't mean those who were not can't succeed.

When using telepathy, it may not be possible to carry out a full conversation with your BFF using just your minds, but you can transmit images, words, or feelings to one another. To start, let your friend know that you want to try communicating with them telepathically. This is important especially when you're beginning because you will both need to be in a relaxed, focused and receptive state. You can try meditating or deep breathing before to prepare so that your body and mind are relaxed.

They don't have to be in the same room or space as you; they can be at their house or even in another town. Close your eyes and try to tune out any background noise or distractions, and really focus your thoughts on your friend. Visualize them clearly in your mind's eye their essence, their presence, details of their physical features. Once you have solidified this visualization of them as if they are almost there with you, visualize the word, image or feeling you want to send to them. Solidify it, make it vivid in your mind's eye. Make it your mind's only focus. Now visualize your friend and visualize communicating this image to your friend. Imagine them receiving your message. They should have their mind open and receptive to your message at this point, and they should be visualizing you in their mind's eye. Once you've done this, relax, and let your message drift to the other person. Let it drift from your mind. At this time, you can relax your energy and focus. When the exercise is complete, follow up with them and ask them what they thought or saw in their mind's eye. Make sure to clarify that they shouldn't force any messages; they should just let their mind flow where it will and keep track of what may pop up.

Don't get discouraged if it doesn't work right away. It will take practice and possibly many tries. This is just one way to begin practicing, but no matter how you practice or whom you practice with, stay relaxed (both physically and mentally) and keep your mind open and receptive for both sending and receiving messages. It's important to be in an environment that is totally comfortable, familiar and relaxing to you, to avoid the risk of distraction or being snapped out of your focus by strange noises, people, smells, etc. When you are just beginning your telepathy journey, and you've just started to practice, the best place to start is in your own home, maybe your bedroom or a room you find particularly relaxing. If your house is hectic and chaotic or you just can't feel relaxed there, try your backyard or a quiet park somewhere in a natural setting. Nature can help ground you and energize your powers. As long as it's a place you can tune out effectively, it should work.

The other commonly known aspect of telepathy is reading the minds of others. Telepathy is harder to practice on strangers, so again first practice with someone you are close with – a willing friend, family member, or partner. When attempting to read their mind, make sure to ask permission. Mind reading won't reveal to you a play by play of what they are thinking, but it will give you a vague idea, sense, or maybe a word or image related to what they are thinking about. Again, the same as with telepathic communication, you want to be in a setting that relaxes you. Close your eyes, tune everything out, and focus your energy on the person whose mind you are trying to read. Get the other person to picture something simple like a banana, and really focus on it. Obviously, they can't tell you what they are thinking. Once they confirm they have solidified their image, visualize them, try and connect with their energy, and let your mind flow.

They do not necessarily have to connect with you or be on the same energy level for this practice because, as opposed to if they were sharing their image with you via telepathic communication, mind reading is more of a one-way street/ one-man job. Make a note of all the things that flowed easily – not forced – through your mind and check in with them to see if you got anything right. Say, for instance, you saw the color yellow, or smelled banana bread, or felt disgusted (maybe they hate bananas). Don't be discouraged if you didn't get anything right the first few times you try this.

An additional way to practice with someone you know is to prepare yourself accordingly but then ask them a question out loud. Tell them not to answer it but just think about and process how they feel about it and what they would answer to it. It can't be a question you know or suspect the answer to. Right after you ask it, they will likely have an immediate reaction and/ or thought, so assuming you're relaxed and your mind is receptive, see what enters your mind immediately after asking the question. Check in with them to see if you accurately picked up on anything.

Once you've built up from these exercises and think you are ready for a challenge, try mind reading next time you're on public transit or in a crowd somewhere. Do this as unobtrusively as you can. If you sense that someone's energy is really blocking you out and doesn't want to let anyone in, they want their privacy. Leave them be and try someone else who's perhaps more receptive. One common thing mind reader pick up on when reading minds are people's emotions. It's probably the easiest thing to access using telepathy, and you've probably read people's emotions telepathically before without even knowing it.

It's important to distinguish body language and facial cues giving you information on someone, and telepathy providing that information. To remain unbiased and make sure telepathy is your only source of information, try to focus on someone's energy rather than looking at them/ their appearance. You may focus on someone, trying to pick something up from them and feel a rush of worry wash over you. You may even pick up the reason why they are worried, though perhaps in a vague sense, and it may take more experience to get this specific.

In a way, mind reading is similar to psychometry. You are trying to pick things up from a person: thoughts, emotions, images, etc. Except you can get a reading from them without actually touching them, which would be especially weird while practicing on a crowd of strangers in public. What's important to remember with telepathy is that patience is key. It is not going to click overnight; in fact, it may take quite a while before you effectively get the hang of it, so don't be hard on yourself if you don't find that you are successful right away. You also may feel energetically drained after a session. Don't draw your practice out for too long as telepathy really works out your brain and it may exhaust you. If a message isn't going through, just plan to try it again another day. Don't deplete your mental power.

And remember when practicing either telepathic communication or mind reading, do not look at that person's face directly (if possible), as facial features and movements may cloud your judgment, mental focus, and force the reading or interpretation. Try to do it as best as possible using only your mind, so if you get it right, you can be sure it was telepathy, and there was no bias involved.

Have you ever thought of someone and then at the exact same time or shortly after you receive a call or message from that very person? This is one common experience of telepathy among people. Telepathy is mind-to-mind communication and is usually much stronger when two individuals share a strong connection. For example, you have probably experienced telepathy with a close best friend or relative. You may say something at the same time or that individual will say exactly what you were thinking.

Some people may say its predictability, but I think that as you grow closer with a person your thoughts naturally become in sync and you will pick up on what that person is thinking without them saying a word. Telepathy is also stronger when the thought or message is emotionally charged rather than just sitting down and trying to send a thought to someone. You will have a higher chance of experiencing telepathy when you are sending an emotionally charged thought or a powerful emotion such as love to someone. Telepathy can also be experienced when thoughts are shared at the same moment or simultaneously. People may experience this with death. A client of mine woke up in the early morning and sensed her long-distance relative passed away. She checked her phone and received a call confirming the relative had just died.

HOW CAN YOU TELL THE DIFFERENCE BETWEEN TELEPATHY AND IMAGINATION?

Telepathic impressions manifest simultaneously or at the exact same time between two people or as spontaneous information about a person or situation. Imagination only comes from within and has no connection to reality. It can also manifest as personal wishful thinking or projection towards someone.

When someone mistakes wishful thinking for telepathy, it is because they want their own personal desires or wishes to be expressed or manifested in reality. Another common mistake for telepathy is projection; where a person puts their own feelings onto someone and believes the other person is experiencing those feelings. People project onto others all the time to avoid taking responsibility for their own actions.

An example of projection confused with telepathy would be a brother who refuses to call his sister after a big argument because he senses she is still mad at him when in reality he is the one who is still angry with her.

Most of us have been in a situation in which auras have been casually brought up in the conversation. Many people are left wondering what an aura is and what they mean. This confusion generally stems from a lack of understanding, and with so many different ideas about what an aura is, this is understandable. However, like most anything else, all it takes is a little education to make things much clearer. If you know about auras, the next time it is brought up in conversation you will have some correct information to share. You might also find that a lot of people will be very curious to hear what you have to say. There are many people interested in auras and aura reading than what you may think. There are still skeptics out there which make some people hesitant to ask questions or seek out information on their own.

On a fundamental level, it is the magnetic field surrounding every living thing that makes up an aura. A person's aura is unique and reflects their own particular energy, it is this energy that impacts their capacity to connect and interact with others. Most people's auras extend about three feet around them, but those who have suffered a tragedy, or a trauma usually have a larger aura. Much of what we do in our lives leaves some type of mark on our aura, that is why experienced readers are able to tell so much about a person during a reading. Our aura is so intimately connected to both our minds and our bodies, that it is difficult to keep secrets from experienced readers. This is why it is good to choose a reader than you think you can trust and that you feel comfortable with.

The study of chakras is an ancient tradition and was often treated more like a visit to a doctor. It was known that the chakras held information about both our mental and physical health, so it would make sense to see someone about chakra alignment if there was an issue. Our auras originate from these chakras and therefore, can also reveal what ails us. Many people believe that getting regular aura readings keeps them healthy because the aura can reflect some diseases or illnesses before more classic symptoms arise, increasing the likelihood of a speedy and full recovery. Experienced aura readers do not even need to meet their subject in person in order to give a proper reading, they can just do it from a normal photograph. That is how deeply connected we are to our auras, they show up in regular photographs, meaning they must be pretty powerful for that to happen. Auras can always change, because they reflect our thoughts and emotions, so while some of the basic traits, both and good and bad remain the same, other aspects of our aura shift along with our moods and circumstances.

An aura is not one single unit lie a sheet, instead, it is made up of many different layers. The aura's layers interconnect and mingle that form the cohesive body that is known as the aura. Each layer of the aura holds different types of information, these are known as the subtle bodies. The energy created by the chakras are what create the auras. The size of a person's aura depends on their spiritual, emotional, and physical health, these auric layers will contract or increase depending on these facets.

THE 7 LAYERS THAT MAKE UP AN AURA

- **The first layer,** also called the etheric layer remains close to the body, generally only extending an inch or two from the body. The etheric field reflects your physical health and is usually different shades blue. This layer will change shade and radius along with your physical health. This layer originates from the root chakra and it is what makes up the link between your physical and higher bodies.
- **The second layer** that is influenced by emotions generally extends only about one to three inches from the body. This layer holds your emotions and feelings, which we all know change on a regular basis depending on your particular circumstances. Usually, this layer is bright and combines many different colors, but negative feelings and emotions can act as a block which can dull or darken the color. The sacral chakra is associated with this layer, which is fitting because it is beneath the heart's location, the figurative source of emotion.
- **The third layer** of the aura is the mental field, and it can spread out from the body anywhere from three to eight inches. The mental layer is generally a shade of yellow, varying from bright to dull. For those suffering from depression or anxiety, this layer is greatly affected. This layer also relates to the solar plexus chakra.
- **The fourth layer** is the astral layer, which acts a bridge to the spiritual realm and is connected to the astral plane. This layer extends about a

foot from the body and contains all the colors of the rainbow, with the brightness correlating with a person's spiritual health. The astral plane is one part of the multi-dimensional planes that surrounds us. This plane vibrates on a higher frequency than the physical plane that we live in. The fourth layer is connected with the heart or fourth chakra and is often referred to as the 'layer of love' for this reason. It also joins the higher three and lower three auric layers.

- **The fifth layer** is called the etheric template, it protrudes around two feet from the body. This layer contains a guideline of the entities in the physical world, and because of this it is not usually associated with a specific color. This layer can also create negative space because it does deal with the physical world, but this is not negative, it just means that many different colors can be associated with it. The throat or fifth chakra is related to this layer and represents your personality and identity.

- **The sixth layer** is also known as the celestial aura and can protrude up to two and a half feet from the body. This layer is also linked to the spiritual realm and any communication with that realm is reflected in this layer. The celestial aura also mirrors feelings of ecstasy and unconditional love. The colors in this layer appear shimmery and are usually pearly pastels. This layer originates from the third eye or sixth chakra, intuition and perception are the focus here.

- **The final layer** can extend up to three feet from the body and is known as the Ketheric layer. This field contains all the other layers and basically, acts as a barrier to hold them together. The Ketheric layer vibrates at the highest frequencies and contains bright gold threads that weave throughout it. This layer reflects the trials and experiences that have made an impact on the soul. The Ketheric layer acts as your own personal connection to the Divine and aids in your journey of being personally connected to the universe. The crown chakra is related to this layer, and it represents our connection with all that exists.

Even though these layers all make up the aura, the first layer itself is not actually the aura, it is the energy that leads to the creation of the aura. This is also known as the Energosma, and the aura really starts where the

Energosma ends, which is why auras can vary in size from person to person and from day to day. As our emotions and thoughts change, so do our auras since they are a manifestation of our over-all health.

One person's aura can also be affected by another person's, this is known as an auric connection and can make communication easier. This happens because the energies from the two people become stronger and take on a greater role in the communication, usually without the people knowing it is even happening. This helps to explain those inexplicable connections we have with some people as if we have known them for years.

When it comes to reading auras, there is no one right way. They all deal with psychic abilities and some people will be more naturally inclined to one or more and may choose to only pursue that which comes easier to them. The ways to read auras include seeing, feeling, and knowing them, they are all similar and even connected in some ways, but all are equally effective. So, when you decide which path to pursue, you might decide to choose feeling because you are someone who already depends on your sense of intuition. Opting to further develop what is already a natural psychic gift will make the process easier since it is already something you have used and at least somewhat developed even if you are not consciously aware of doing so.

Just like the human body, auras are complex. They are direct reflections of how we feel at any given time. Even if we are not aware of it, our auras can show those capable of reading them how we are feeling about our lives and how our past experiences have impacted us. As we grow and evolve, so will our aura, since it is basically a mirror of what we are feeling on the inside. This means that if you want a brighter aura there are things you can do to make that happen.

Interpreting dreams to find their relevance in physical life, Empaths often are lucid dreamers. This can be proof of how strong your spiritual side is. This means that there is an ability to shift through dimensions and connect with energies that are beyond the limits of normal understanding.

Free-fall dreams are also common for Empaths. These types of dreams connect with releasing spiritual energies. They also are up to interpretation because many believe that it means strength to stand up for themselves in waking life must be found. Sequential dreams can be very structured and events in the dreams can be connected. This chronicles events used to bring an understanding of a potential real-life event.

Creative dreams can come across as sources of inspiration. Empaths can get ideas from their dream worlds and bring them into their lives. Having vivid imaginations and lots of experience with multiple forms of energy, Empaths can experience very creative and vivid dream worlds. Nightmares can be very disturbing and haunting to Empaths. Because they are sensitive beings even the smallest details can settle into a permanent place in their minds until they resolve them. Performing sleep meditations and energy-clearing techniques before resting can help to bring forth positive dreams.

Having the ability to process and deal with the emotional stress that intense dreams can bring forth is important for Empaths. Most of them will be able to define dreams with clarity and understand when their dreams are mirroring their subconscious and spiritual realities. Before realizing that one is an Empath, it's quite easy for them to go through life as an unsuspecting energy sponge. Those that are unaware of their abilities will take on these emotions and energies everywhere they go without understanding why. This can lead to suddenly feeling sick or becoming overwhelmed with anxiety or sadness even when there is nothing around to cause this feeling. You must develop specific self-care skills and protection techniques to manage your empathic nature and prevent overload. Bringing awareness into your body becomes extremely important. Find activities and exercises that bring you back into your body and the present moment. As an Empath, you may experience nervous system overdrive, and it's important that you notice the signs and take the steps to remedy them. Breathing techniques that bring the heart rate down and return to your baseline. Be careful to take stock of how you feel after you spend time with others. It won't take long to learn what people and situations are hazardous to your well-being.

One method of self-care for Living as an Empath is to get in touch with and unblock your chakras. If you are familiar with the 7 Chakras, you understand how you can manage the energy and emotions in your body through them. In just a few minutes a day, you can clear all stored energy and strengthen all these energetic centers. An easy way to do this is to concentrate on a Chakra while meditating and perform breathing exercises, visualizing that you are pulling clear, clean energy into the area and breathing out all negative, and stored energies from the area. There are many stretches that focus on balancing and aligning Chakras, and Yoga can be extremely helpful for Empaths who are feeling overwhelmed. Unblock energies and keep them flowing freely.

COMMON DREAMS AND THEIR INTERPRETATION

DREAMS ABOUT FALLING

Most of us have dreamt about falling from great heights at least once in our lives. It is a very common and scary dream and some people believe that you should not hit the ground in this dream because you will die. Of course, this is just a myth and there is no truth in it!

So, what does it mean?

Dream experts have linked this dream with problems in the dreamer's life. They say that it is a sign that something is getting out of control. It means that you need to amend the choices you have made or take a different direction in some parts of your life. It could also signify fear and anxiety that you have over a certain situation in your life like in your place of work or your relationship.

DREAM ABOUT BEING LATE

Have you ever dreamt of being late and missing some opportunities? This dream can be very stressful and frustrating. This symbolizes the anxieties that you have in your life. You could be scared about upcoming changes or you are worried if you can finish the projects that you are working on. If you dream of being late for appointments or dates, then it means that you are overwhelmed by work such that you do not have enough time for yourself. If it is about getting late for the airport and missing a flight, then it means your time is not enough for you to finish what you are doing. Therefore, the best remedy for this is just to take enough work that you can handle.

DREAMS ABOUT WANTING TO USE THE BATHROOM BUT YOU CAN'T FIND THE TOILET

Dreaming about looking for a toilet when we want to use it can be frustrating. In this dream, you may find that when you try to relieve yourself somewhere you find that some people are looking at you. The feeling here can be shameful yet the call of nature is pushing you to find a place. Dream experts suggest that this could be a representation of the anxieties and fear that we are having in our lives. It could also be a sign that we are not allowing ourselves the basic needs in our lives. It means that we are too busy attending to the needs of other people that we forget our own needs. It could also mean that we have a problem in expressing ourselves in our waking life.

DREAMING ABOUT SNAKES

Dreaming of seeing snakes or being bitten by them can be very frightening. Most of us have had this dream at some point in our lives, so what does it mean? This dream has a different interpretation for different people and different situations. This could signify some worries or fears in your waking life that require attention. However, most dream experts suggest that this dream symbolizes temptations, danger, and forbidden sexuality. Snakes symbolize healing and transformation and it can be a sign of warning that something bad will happen. Being chased by snakes means that you are running from something that needs your attention.

If the snake chasing you is a wild one, then it signifies that something in your life is getting out of control and this could be your health or relationship. If the dream is about fighting with a snake, then it means that you are opposing some changes or situations in your life. This could be something that you do not want to happen or something, which happened, but you do not like it. If you dream of a snake biting you, then it means you are facing hard times, which can destroy you so you need to take action immediately.

DREAMS ABOUT TAKING AN EXAM

This is a very common dream for those people who are out of school and those people who work in performance-related jobs. It is associated with self-criticism and the desire to achieve higher expectations in life. Dream interpreters claim that this dream signifies anxiety and fear of failure. It can also symbolize an upcoming event that requires you to make decisions or a new phase in your life. It could also mean that you are suffering from low self-esteem or low self-confidence and you fear that you are not handling life challenges the way you should.

DREAMS ABOUT BEING PREGNANT

This is another dream that has multiple interpretations.it symbolizes new beginnings and new challenges. Loewenberg a dream expert believes that this is a positive dream and it symbolizes some growth and development in woman's potential. It also represents the birth of a new idea, direction, or project. It could also represent a woman's fear of becoming an inadequate mother in her parenting. This dream is associated with an increase in finances, the flowering of romance, great change.

DREAMS ABOUT FLYING

Dreams about flying can be fascinating at the same time scary if you fear great heights. This dream has had different interpretations. Some dream experts suggest that it represents freedom and independence and it could mean that you are trying to escape from some situations in your life.

Other dream experts claim that if you are unable to fly in this dream, it means that you are straining to achieve your set goals, or something is preventing you from reaching your target in life. They suggest that flying alone represents independence and freedom from social restraints or you have released yourself from those things that have been weighing you down.

DREAMS ABOUT A CHEATING PARTNER

This dream can be very worrying, and it can make someone ask himself or herself the question of "what if it's true?" so what's the deeper meaning of this distressing dream for couples?

Dream experts suggest that having such dreams does not mean that your partner is cheating or will cheat. It could be reflections of the fear you have for infidelity or maybe you have been cheated on before and you fear that it might happen again. You could be testing the limits of reality! Such dreams also symbolize that there are trust issues in your relationship and there is a gap in communication. Not spending enough time with your partner because of job commitments or distance can also lead to such dreams. It could also be a sign that something needs correction in your relationship.

DREAMS ABOUT LOSING TEETH

This kind of dream has different interpretations. Some dream experts believe that teeth symbolize power and confidence so the dream could mean that the dreamer has lost confidence and the ability to be assertive and decisive maybe because of what happened in their lives. To some, it is a sign of a broken relationship, a fulfillment of becoming pregnant, and it could mean sexual stimulation for men. Some interpreters also suggest that this dream could signify doubt about one's attractiveness and appearance. It could also represent anxiety about communicating something or fear that one might have said something embarrassing.

DREAMS ABOUT BEING NAKED IN PUBLIC

It can be frustrating to dream that you are showing up in your workplace or school naked! Dream experts suggest that this kind of dream represents feelings of vulnerability, insecurity, shame, and humiliation. This is common for individuals who have landed a new job that involves coming into public view.

DREAMS ABOUT DYING

This is a horrifying dream and most people will wake up from the dream crying. You can dream about the death of your relative or a friend. Some people believe that if you keep such dreams to yourself it would happen! However, this is not true. Dream interpreters suggest that this dream signifies anxiety about change. It can happen if you are scared of changes because you do not know what will happen on the other side of change. Therefore, it is simply the mourning of the inevitable passage of time. This dream could also mean that the dreamer wishes to end something bothering them in their life. This could be a stressful job, relationship, or a past that is haunting them. Some experts believe that this is not a dream but an encouragement to pursue new endeavors.

DREAMS ABOUT BEING CHASED

Have you ever dreamt of being chased by the unknown attacker, but you feel your legs are heavy and slowing you down? This is a very common and terrifying dream.

What is its deeper meaning? Dream experts claim that this dream means that you have some things you are trying to run from in your life. It could be a desire to escape from your fears!

If you dream that you are being attacked but you cannot run no matter how much you try, then it signifies that you are suffering from low self-esteem and low self-confidence. It could also mean that you are in a situation that you are powerless.

The interpretation of this dream will depend on the identity of the attacker. If it is an animal, then it could mean you are running from your own emotions and passions. If it is an unknown attacker then it signifies your fears of your childhood abuses and trauma and if the attacker is someone from the opposite sex, then you are afraid of love. This could be a result of an abusive past relationship.

In the westernized societies, if a person comes down with an illness, a physician is the answer. Modern medicine is useful, yes, but there's even a more potent curative technique known as spiritual healing. This practice is relatively new and hasn't gained wide acceptance yet, but its practitioners know that it works. Spiritual healing is not concerned about alleviating a single disease but restoring wholesome health to an individual.

Spiritual healers have known of their potential since they were little. Empaths tend to have an inherent capacity to become spiritual healers. The following are some signs that indicate you have the potential of becoming a spiritual healer:

YOU ALMOST NEVER GET SICK

You seem to radiate an energy that keeps you from falling ill. You don't remember ever going to the hospital to receive drugs or an injection. You have always had perfect health.

Although you live a normal life like everybody else, you seem not to be affected by the disease-causing germs that affect other people.

YOU HAVE AN ODD ABILITY TO PERCEIVE PATTERNS

It has always seemed that you can unravel a pattern to most things that happen in your life or other people's lives. Ever since you were little, these patterns have just been obvious to you, and other people consider you weird for being able to do that.

YOU FEEL CONNECTED TO ANIMALS

You have never understood people who treat animals cruelly. You have such a special bond with animals, and it is almost as though you can communicate with them. You have kept various pets ever since you were little and particularly keep cats or dogs as pets.

YOU ATTRACT CHILDREN

It is almost as though children are magnetized toward you. It doesn't matter whether the children are not familiar with you, they will still come running and crash into you. Children are very excited around you. And they seem to hang on your every word. They have elevated you into a figure of authority.

YOU AVOID CROWDS

Crowded areas like shopping malls and nightclubs seem to give you a mini heart attack. The noise produced by all those people sucks the peace out of you. Being surrounded by many people tends to drain your energy. This causes you to actively avoid being caught up in crowds.

YOU CAN SENSE WEATHER CHANGE

You tend to instinctively know how the day's weather will pan out. It could be raining now, and your guts tell you that there will be sunshine some other time, and true, the sun shines later. Being sensitive to weather patterns is a rare gift, and if you possess it, you are definitely an energy healer.

PEOPLE FLOCK TO YOU FOR HELP

People trust you for answers. People you barely know often come up to you and 'pour their hearts out'. They seem to think that you have their answers. They ask for advice about dealing with life's frustrations. And just as they hoped, you play that role perfectly well.

YOU'RE A VERY GOOD LISTENER

You have realized that listening is one of your strong traits. People can go on and on without giving you a chance to talk, and you're in the least bit bothered. This ability of yours allows you to be patient enough to let people reveal as much as they can about themselves. Your hobbies are worlds apart from your peers' hobbies Perhaps your peers are into playing Ping-Pong, beach partying, or even sports. However, you have zero interest in mainstream hobbies. Your hobbies include things like yoga or reading novels. Your interest in non-mainstream hobbies has made you less visible amongst your peers.

YOUR DREAMS COME TRUE

Everything that you ever saw in your dreams came to pass. Various elements in your dreams might be symbolic, but you will still have the insight of getting the message.

This ability has bestowed on your precognitive powers. You seem to know what the future holds.

YOU HAVE ENDURED A TRAUMATIC EVENT

Maybe you had a sad childhood, and it scarred you for life. The trauma was critical in awakening your spiritual healing capability though. As you have matured, you have consigned the trauma in your past and are thriving at present.

But from time to time, the memories appear in the back of your head.

YOU DON'T FEEL A SENSE OF BELONGING

You have gone to many places and done many things, but you have never quite felt home. You feel like an alien from another planet. You haven't quite met someone that you could call a kindred spirit. Yes, the basic decency is there, but you cannot connect with other people at a primal level.

At the start, it used to bother you, but not anymore.

ELECTROMAGNETIC HYPERSENSITIVITY

This has made you feel very weird about yourself. When you are around some object radiating electromagnetic signals, you tend to affect its normal functioning. For instance, you might walk into a room and the lights blink, or you may touch a radio, and it suddenly dies down.

YOU ALWAYS ATTRACT PEOPLE WHO NEED TO BE SAVED

Looking back at all the people who came into your life, you are startled to realize that they needed something from you. They needed to be saved. And you did a great job of saving them – or at least tried to.

YOU HAVE WITNESSED NUMEROUS MYSTICAL ACTIVITIES

Deep inside you know that there's more to life than we presently know. You have on various occasions experienced supernatural events that left you baffled. Maybe you were asleep and felt a weird presence in your room, or maybe you have actually seen an entity that can be described as otherworldly. You just know that there is a lot of mystical stuff out there that we haven't figured out yet.

Meditation relaxes your body and mind and helps you to focus. Meditation plays an important role in opening your third eye. Different types of meditation will work differently for everybody. It's important to do this on a regular basis to achieve your awareness of your third eye. Here some important rules for your meditation practice.

- You need an appropriate space. It needs to be in an area where there are no distractions, where you will have maximum focus. It doesn't have to be completely soundproof. A separate room in your house that you reserve solely for your meditation. You can't meditate in a room where the TV is on, or cars are roaring by.
- Do some stretch to loosen and warm up your muscles.
- Find a posture where you can meditate the best. The most common postures are lotus or half lotus. Sit with your legs crossed and your hands on your knees. Make sure you keep you back straight and stay alert. You can close your eyes but don't get sleepy. You can stay alerted without being tense.
- Once your body is relaxed, start to calm you mind. Clear your mind from all thoughts, letting it relax. Listen to the little sounds around you and focus on your breath. Notice how it feels when you breathe. All meditation must involve the process of clearing your mind.
- Stay calm and determined. It will require daily practice to meditate properly. Don't give up. Stay firm and keep reverting your mind back to the current task.
- Focus on the third eye position as you block out all your thoughts. As you focus you will see a point of light appear. Focus on this light. Visualize it spreading.
- Don't think while you focus on the light. Keep breathing and concentrating.
- Let the light become brighter and send more light out.
- The more you practice this, the more your body will become relaxed. This will allow the third eye to open more.
- Allow the light to envelop and fill your body and soul as you connect to your high state.
- Thoughts may pop into your mind, let them unfold and go away.

- When the feeling starts to disappear, pull yourself back to the present. Don't push yourself, let it happen slowly.
- Take a few deep breaths and become aware of your body and surroundings.

CHANTING

- Start as before and continue breathing. Once you get rid of all distractions and can stay focused on your breathing, move to the next step.
- Perform the Shambhavi mudra. Turn your eyes upward toward the third eye chakra. Look but don't strain your eyes. Try to get your eyes in position while staying relaxed.
- Take a deep breath in through your nose while keeping your mouth closed. Place the tip of your tongue between your teeth and bite down gently.
- Breathe out through your mouth. Chant "thoh" while doing this. This will send a vibration to the third eye. The "th" should vibrate as you do this. Now focus on opening your third eye.
- The tone of the vibration needs to be in "a", "b", or "c".
- Don't rush. Do the breathing and chanting slow and steady. Your lungs are ready to receive the air for your next deep breath.
- You will feel the vibration in the center of your forehead. Your thoughts should all be positive. Think about love and compassion.
- Exhale and take another deep breath. Exhale and chant again. Repeat this about five times. Do this exercise regularly for a few days. You will gain more focus on the third eye meditation. You will notice a slight pressure at your third eye.
- Do this for five days and move on to the next step.
- Erect posture in the lotus position again.
- Regular breathing exercises. Deep breath in through the nose and out slowly through your mouth. Exhale all the negativity inside out. Imagine all this coming out with your breath. You should feel cleansed from all the stress.
- Do the Shambhavi mudra and focus on the third eye.

- See the color indigo at the third eye and feel how positive and bright it is.
- Do a "c" tone chant and feel the vibrations at your chakra. This will keep the chakra stimulated.
- Think of all the positive things you want in life. Don't think of anything in particular. Let the picture come to you. Once you realize what it is it will give you true happiness.
- Repeat every day after opening your chakra. The third eye needs stimulation to stay active and balanced. Once you've built a strong foundation you will become more receptive to higher things.
- Opening the third eye takes a lot of time and determination. Lots of discipline is needed to achieve this state of consciousness. Results will not come fast. It has been said that people who were spiritually awakened in a previous life will be able to open their third eye faster in this life.
- Time will vary from person to person. It can take years trying to meditate properly without allowing distractions. You will need to get rid of all blockages to be able to open the third eye.

WORK WITH DIRECT INSTINCT EXECISE

Direct instinct, likewise, called exacting instinct, is the kind of instinct you outfit when you get some information about a particular situation.

Now get ready...

Start to hear the noise around you...

Breathe in... Breathe out...

Close your eyes...

Breathe again...

Breathe in ... Breath out...

Breathe in ... Breath out...

Breathe in ... Breath out...

Make yourself agreeable...

Plunk down in a tranquil spot and center your breathing until your body unwinds.

Breathe in ... Breath out...

Breathe in ... Breath out...

Breathe in ... Breath out...

Distinguish a circumstance you might want knowledge on.

Concentrate on this circumstance for a few minutes.

Approach so anyone might hear or in your brain for a direct natural encounter about it sooner rather than later.

Release it.

You may need to do this on different occasions before anything happens to it, however by concentrating your vitality on one explicit circumstance, your instinct is bound to get on prompts for that circumstance than on whatever else.

Breathe in ... Breath out... Release it...

Breathe in ... Breath out... Release it...

Breathe in ... Breath out... Release it...

Keep your eyes closed...

Work on your circuitous instinct...

Roundabout instinct, additionally called representative instinct, centers around the mind's normal capacity to get on things of key significance by building up your capacity to see in and decipher mental images.

You're almost ready ...

Ask yourself, "**What does my life need at the present time?**"

Repeat this inquiry multiple times, while envisioning yourself moving to a progressively important answer each time.

You are ready...

Open your eyes...

Snatch a pencil and a bit of paper...

In the wake of posing the inquiry multiple times, get your pencil and draw the main image that rings a bell...

Decipher the image...

Make sense of what it speaks to from your viewpoint and how that idea plays into your life...

Tune in to your fantasies...

You can do this exercise at any place or time of day ...

The human personality enters the REM phase of rest at regular intervals, and during this time, the mind dreams.

Dreams can be an incredible asset in your voyage to decipher signals from outer boosts that your intuitive has as of now analyzed.

Prior to resting, put a stack of paper and a pen by your bed. Ask yourself an inquiry or spotlight on a particular circumstance in your life that you need an instinctive response to. Rehash it as frequently as conceivable before nodding off. When you wake up, record anything you envisioned about. In the event that you didn't dream about anything, compose or draw whatever enters your psyche.

Rehash as required until you find a solution to your inquiry or circumstance.

ATTEMPT A VISUALLY IMPAIRED PERUSING

Daze readings utilize an arrangement of cards to enable you to center your vitality and intuitively answer addresses utilizing your intuition.

Take a seat at a work area with three clear cards.

Consider an inquiry or circumstance you need your instinct to assist you with.

Compose three unique answers for that question, doling out one to each card.

Flip the cards over so the appropriate responses face down.

Mix them and spot them face-down on the work area.

Run your hands over the cards.

Take as much time as necessary, unwind, and inhale profoundly.

Flip the cards over.

The card you felt most attracted to ought to be the right arrangement.

Is it accurate to say that you are natural and insightful about other individuals?

Do you frequently realize what individuals are thinking or feeling before they state anything so anyone can hear?

Do you ever observe hues, shapes, images or an atmosphere around individuals' heads?

Do you now and then 'hear' the responses to questions you ask in consideration or reflection?

On the off chance that you can answer yes to any of these inquiries, you're getting to your 'clairsenses'.

The reality of the situation is, we as a whole have these capacities. Similarly, that we as a whole can see, hear, feel, smell and taste. Presently the facts demonstrate that a few of us have constrained sight or hearing or have a lessened feeling of smell or taste. However, we as a whole know, these capacities are a piece of how we experience and edge our reality.

TRAIN YOUR SENSES

On the off chance that you needed to turn into a wine or espresso authority, you'd figure out how to refine your sense of taste, build up your nose, and well on the way to improve your capacity to see and recognize the various notes, tones and surfaces that rouse and touch off your adoration. Our five faculties are trainable, and with exertion and practice, can turn out to be very developed and exact.

Preparing and exertion can likewise be applied to creating and refining your Clair senses.

CHAPTER 9: GUIDED MEDITATION TO HELP YOUR THIRD EYE TO OPEN

Before starting…

The days following your first opening, meditate a lot and continue to practice the technique until you have perfected it. During the first meditation stages, you will be introduced and helped to transcend states while also building your third eye. It will also help you to silence your mind, so you have complete control over it.

Welcome to your third eye open meditation guided meditation…

Let's start…

Remove all forms of restrictive clothing and jewelry…

Breathe in… Breath out…

Sit in a chair or on the floor with your back straight and legs crossed…

Close and keep your eyes shut throughout the meditation…

Create friction at the back of your throat as you breathe…

Breathe in… Breath out…

Breathe in… Breath out…

Breathe in… Breath out…

Adjust your back to ensure you are upright, and the neck, head, and back are in a straight line…

Create absolute stillness and tranquility…

Become aware of the tingling between your eyebrows…

Connect the vibration in your throat with the vibration between your eyebrows…

The vibration in your throat will help to build the vibration between your eyebrows…

Stop focusing on your throat vibration and turn your attention to the haze, color or glow forming between your eyebrows...

This manifestation is spiritual and it's important that you don't try to imagine the presence of them...

Let the vibration in your throat connect to your manifestation...

As you become more aware of your manifestation, drop your focus from the throat vibration...

Find and focus on the vivid parts of the manifestation and ignore the hazy aspects...

Focus on the background of your manifestation...

This should make it feel like space is opening and extending in front of you...

Drop the throat vibration completely and allow yourself to be absorbed in by this new space...

Let yourself spiral clockwise and forward as if you were falling and spinning into space...

Allow yourself to be caught in the space...

Space will change as you fall, and you will move into a different reality...

Focus on the area above your head completely...

Lose everything, do nothing except for being aware...

Don't move, just let the awareness take over...

Start to listen to the sounds around you...

Bring your attention back to all your body...

Pay attention to your toes and start moving them...

Pay attention to your neck and start moving it...

Pay attention to the fingers of your hands and start moving them...

Open gently your eyes...

Inhale deeply and slowly drift back to full consciousness...

Welcome back and Namaste...

CHAPTER 10: BEST TECHNIQUE ON ASTRAL TRAVEL

Psychics say the mind that dreams hold the astral body, and this causes sudden jerks that wake you up or falling dreams. Many dreams aren't remembered and thus causes astral travel to be a subject of individuality. Those who believe in astral travel will often mention that ghost sightings are typically described as transparent apparitions that walk along the earth.

It isn't clear if every object has an astral counterpart or if the spirit just incarnates into a body and this results in the astral travel. The phenomena might be something entirely different. Astral travel deals a little about life and the things that happen after death.

There are two different thoughts on the nature of astral travel. A broad definition of these would be a phasing model and mystical model.

The Phasing Model believes that it's possible to leave your body. The astral plane and the physical world are both areas of our conscious spectrum. When someone chooses to project, they are phasing into a different area of consciousness and the locations there. You can compare this to changing the radio station. This viewpoint is seen as the external reality is only a state that is created internally.

The Mystical Mode has many astral maps and belief systems but are connected to the beliefs that Astral travel happens outside the physical body. An energy body is thought to carry the consciousness out of the physical body.

Higher planes are reached by progressive projections of subtle energy bodies from other projected bodies. This body is connected to the physical one through an energetic connection that looks like a silver cord some refer to as an umbilical cord.

There are hundreds possibly thousands of techniques to help your astral travel. Everybody is different, so something works for one may not work for another. Try one and if it doesn't work for you, move to a different one.

Welcome to your *Rope Technique* guided meditation...

Lie down on your bed

Close your eyes... and gently fill your lungs with fresh air...

Feel it inside...

Take a deep breath again...

Welcome to this rope technique guided meditation...

Picture a rope hanging off the ceiling...

Imagining this rope helps you to provide pressure on your astral body...

Imagining this rope colored...

Imagining this rope shining...

Reach out with your imagined hands and pull on yourself.

Now breathe again...

Imagining your astral hand...

Look at your astral hands ...

They are colored...

They are shining...

Your hands are like the rope...

Pull yourself hand over hand up the rope that is above you.

You may experience dizziness.

Do not be afraid...

Let go...

You are safe on your bed...

Follow your hands ...

Continue to climb...

You will start to feel the vibration...your entire body will feel like it is vibrating...

You may end up feeling paralyzed... but remember... You are safe on your bed...

Focus completely on the climb...

And goes on... and do not stop...

You don't feel tired...

Infinite energy flows through your soul...

Your astral body is free...

Feel yourself being freed from your body... your astral body...

Now slow down ...

Your astral body will leave the physical in the rope's direction...

You will now notice that you are hovering above your body...

Now you are free...

Enjoy this position for a few minutes...

Remember to breathe...

Remember how you feel...

You smile... you are happy and excited...

When you feel ready you can begin the descent...

Put your hands on your belly...

Feel your breath...

Feel your hands rise and fall to the rhythm of your breathing...

Imagining your return...

Come back to your body...

Now... don't wait...

Welcome back...

Start to move your toes...

Touch with your physical hands your legs...

When you feel ready, open your eyes and enjoy your life...

....

A little suggestion for you:

- Practice this regularly for one month...

Welcome to your *Watch Yourself Sleep* guided meditation...

Lie down... and make sure you're comfortable on your back...

Take it easy...

Look towards the ceiling...

Look at the color of the ceiling... feel the color ...

Look at the imperfections... focus on them...

Feel completely relax... and allow your mind to let go of unwanted thoughts...

Let yourself know that you are going to watch yourself fall asleep...

You will have to be clear about your intents...

Let the body sleep while your mind stays alerted...

Tell yourself to keep consciousness while your body is going into a trance...

My body is sleeping... but my mind is careful...

I feel my body heavy and relaxed... but my mind is alert...

Just focus on this for a few moments...

Once you feel completely relax, become familiar with the sensations that your body has,as you fall asleep...

Don't be afraid of your body...

Don't be afraid of your feelings...

Don't be afraid to feel these new sensations...

Please be aware while this happens... you will feel your body feels numb and heavy...

Pay all your attention to your body's sensations...

You might feel like you are floating or swaying...

You might feel tingling sensations in certain areas...

You could even feel vibrations surging through your entire body...

You may even have buzzing in your ears... but whatever you feel, don't panic... as these are signals that you are on the right path...

Now you are ready...

You need to visualize you are rising from your bed and float to the ceiling...

Hold this image...

You will notice that you are floating above your body...

Relax... everything works...

Don't be afraid of your body...

Don't be afraid of your feelings...

Don't be afraid to feel these new sensations...

Remember to breathe...

Remember how you feel...

You smile... you are happy and excited...

When you feel ready you can start to wake up...

Put your hands on your belly...

Feel your breath...

Feel your hands rise and fall to the rhythm of your breathing...

Imagining your return...

Come back to your body...

Now... don't wait...

Welcome back...

Start to move your toes...

Touch with your physical hands your legs...

When you feel ready, open your eyes and enjoy your life...

…. … …

A little suggestion for you:

- Practice this for 3o minutes.
- You will notice that you are floating above your body, how will it feel if you did float? Make this experience as you can.

Sit or lie down ... it is important that you feel comfortable and at ease...

Welcome to your *Out of Body Experience* guided meditation...

Close your eyes...

Now try to get yourself to go to sleep without falling asleep...

It's important that you are completely relaxed ...

You star to relax...

Pay attention to your body...

Pay attention to my voice...

Now I count from ten to one...

Follow my voice to a deep state of relaxation...

Your body will remain motionless and relaxed... but your mind will be alert and careful...

You will not be afraid... remember that you are safe on your bed...

Ten... feel the weight of your body... nine...

Eight... release the weight of your body... seven...

Six... feel the weight of your arms... five...

Four... release the weight of your arms... three...

Two... you feel free from the weight of your body...

One... feel your state of relaxation... be in a relaxed state....

Pay attention to my voice again...

Keep an awareness of being between awake and asleep...

Let this state deepen and release all of your bad thoughts…

Now peer through your eyelids into the blackness…

Now relax deeper….

Bring vibrations into your body…

Make them become more intense… and continue to control and grow these more…

Now you feel light … follow this feeling …

Inhale gently… and now exhale hard… right now, your astral body leaves your physical body…

Feel proud… feel strong… feel safe…

Next roll yourself over, and you will see the physical body below you…

You can go wherever you want…

I'll leave you a few minutes to explore new places…

Now pay attention to my voice… I'm counting from one to ten…

Follow my voice to an energetic waking state…

Your body will begin to vibrate with new energy… and your mind will be alert and careful…

One… feel your state of relaxation… be a relaxed state…

Two… you begin to be aware of the weight of your arms… three…

Four… regain control of your arms and slowly begin to move them… five…

Six… you begin to be aware of the weight of your body… seven…

Eight … regain control of your body… nine… ten…

Pay attention to my voice again...

Put your hands on your belly...

Feel your breath...

Feel your hands rise and fall to the rhythm of your breathing...

Imagining your return...

Welcome back...

Start to move your toes...

Touch with your physical hands your legs...

When you feel ready, open your eyes and enjoy your life...

....

A little suggestion for you:

- Practice this for 3o minutes a day
- Keep an awareness of being between awake and asleep, this is what they refer to as a hypnagogic state.

Lucid dreams are where the dreamer is aware of dreaming. In the lucid dream, the person is already outside their body.

. Become obsessed with out of body experiences, and you desire it. It's important that you read as much about it as you can. You need to think about it constantly.

. When your mind is ridden with thoughts of out of body experiences, you need affirmations and triggers so you can have lucid dreams.

. All day long think about having a lucid dream.

. The reality tests. Ask yourself if you are dreaming now. You will be able to program your subconscious to make a lucid dream possible.

. Once you're in one of these dreams, and you aware of it, begin to notice that you are no longer in your body. You will be able to make yourself to see your bedroom.

. When you do this, your dream world will disappear, and you will find yourself floating about your body.

. Practice this every day and observe what happens about your life. This helps you to have memories to use in the lucid dreams.

Part II
Empath

CHAPTER 1: WHAT IS AN EMPATH AND HOW TO RECOGNIZE IT

An empath is a person with the special gift of perceiving the emotions and feelings of other people as though they were their own. They don't even try. They are naturally tuned in to the energies floating around them. If an empath walks into a room and sits next to a person who's quietly mourning, the empath will pick up on the sorrow and experience it as though it were their own. An empath who lacks awareness of their gift can be deeply conflicted, as they cannot tell apart their own feelings from those of others.

It can be awesome having the ability to pick up on other people's energies, but on the downside, it can be a real struggle when the said energies are of the dark nature and especially if the empath in question knows nothing of their ability.

As an empath, these are some traits that you're bound to display:

HIGHLY SENSITIVE

People keep on telling you that you're too sensitive. This is because what they say or do can affect you quite easily. You can read into their unsaid messages when they talk or do something. This sensitivity can make you susceptible to things that don't hurt well-adjusted people.

Your high sensitivity makes you give a lot of thought to what you do or say. This pattern always leads to self-inhibiting tendencies. You end up customizing yourself too much so that the world can fall in love with you. The habit of suppressing your true emotions comes with a cocktail of challenges.

SOAK UP OTHER PEOPLES' ENERGIES

You could be having a fantastic day with your spirits high, and then you go to Starbucks and sit next to a family who unbeknownst to you just lost one of their members. Nothing is said. All are sipping at their coffee with quiet faces. Ever so slowly, the joy you first had begins to fade away, and in its place, sadness takes over. You have no reason to be sad, but you experience this sadness anyway. Soon, the family gets up, troops out of Starbucks, and then your sadness fades away. You had just absorbed their energies.

INTROVERTED

Being introverted is not the same as being shy. A shy person might loathe being alone and feel rejected for lack of human contact, but on the other hand, an introvert gets drained when they stay too long with other people, and they cherish being alone. A shy person has self-inhibiting tendencies, but an introvert has a strong sense of self and stays true to it. Empaths are more likely to be introverted than extroverted. They don't shun all human contact but prefer socializing on one-on-one terms, or within small groups.

HIGHLY INTUITIVE

One of the most effective weapons in an empath's hands is their gut feeling. They have this ability to sniff out the true nature of a situation. This makes it a bit hard to play games with an empath. They will see right through your tricks. As an empath, if you meet someone, you tend to have a gut feeling of what that person is really like. You are always in tune with your surroundings and can tell when there's danger. This ability is obviously one of the main advantages of being an empath because you're less likely to be taken for a ride.

OVERWHELMED BY RELATIONSHIPS

Conventional relationships put emphasis on partners spending as much time together as possible. An empath cannot thrive in this kind of arrangement because they constantly pick up on their partner's emotions and mistake them as their own. This is not to say that empaths cannot form any relationships. However, the traditional arrangement of a relationship needs to be deconstructed. For instance, they can have a room of their own that they may retreat to when their urge to be alone kicks in, and also, their partners should be patient with them.

TAKE LONG TO PROCESS EMOTIONS

The average person has a laser attention to their emotions. Whether sadness or joy, it kicks in suddenly. Their emotional reflexes are fast too. An empath takes the time to understand the emotions that they are currently feeling. For instance, if something terrible goes down, the sadness won't register immediately. They will first try to process the situation, going over the details time and again, and then the sadness will well up inside them. They can experience emotions in such a powerful way. Thus, whether it's sadness or joy, they feel it to the full.

LOVE NATURE

For most empaths, they are at their happiest when surrounded by nature. Whether it's the sunlight kissing their skin, the rain falling on them, or taking in a gulp of fresh air, no other activity restores their balance as being surrounded by the natural world. They feel a deep sense of connection with nature. When an empath is experiencing a tsunami of emotions, one of the restorative measures would be taking a stroll through an open area beneath the sky.

STRONG SENSES

An empath boasts of very developed senses. They can catch the slightest whiff of an odor, can see into the shadows, can hear the tiniest sound, and can feel the vibrations of various other things. These developed senses make them so good at noticing the small stuff. Empaths seem to notice what would ordinarily escape the attention of most people. For this reason, they tend to flourish in careers that demand close attention and the exploration of the abstract.

GENEROUS

There isn't a more selfless person than an empath. They don't have to have something in order to help. They are willing to go the extra mile and be of help. For instance, when an empath comes across a street child and sees their suffering, it tugs at their heart. They not only want to give them some food but also find a way of removing them from the streets. The majority of the world doesn't care about street children and see them as an annoyance. We can assume that the empaths of the world play a critical role in helping street children and other people who are experiencing hardship.

CREATIVE

Empaths tend to be very creative. This is aided by the wealth of emotions that they are always experiencing. Their creative nature manifests itself in almost every aspect of their life — food, relationships, homes, and most importantly, career. An empath is likely to do well in a career in the arts. They have tremendous potential when it comes to drawing, writing, singing, or making films. They tend to portray their emotions unambiguously and can capture the emotions of other people just as intended.

PEOPLE ARE DRAWN TO YOU

If an empath isn't aware of their special gift, they are likely to hide away from the world. They would rather hide and be safe than stay among people and experience every emotion imaginable. This can make the society grow suspicious of them and even hate them. However, if an empath is self-aware and knows of their ability to soak up the energies floating around them, then people will be drawn to them. People know that empaths have a tremendous capacity of understanding them and helping them get through whatever challenges they are facing.

EMPATHS FALL INTO THE FOLLOWING DISTINCT CATEGORIES

- **Geomantic empaths**: These empaths are attuned to a certain environment or landscape. Geomantic empaths are connected to specific sites like buildings, lakes, oceans, and mountains. These empaths can feel the historical emotions of these sites. For instance, if an empath visits a site where people were slaughtered many years, they can still feel the sorrow. Empaths attach feelings to different environments so that each environment evokes certain emotions.

Such empaths tend to carry souvenirs to remind them of various environments.

- **Physical empaths**: Also known as a medical empath, they can pick up on the condition of someone else's body. They would instinctively know what ails another person. In extreme cases, they can pick up on the symptoms so that they share in the pain of the other person. Physical empaths also have healing abilities. They tend to take careers in conventional or alternative medicine. Physical empaths are great at taking care of ailing people. Those who have ailments trust them instinctively because they can feel that they care.

- **Emotional empaths**: They are sensitive to the emotional energy floating around them. As an emotional empath, you will absorb the emotions of other people and think that they are yours. This can be deeply distressing if you're constantly around negative people. An emotional empath should increase their self-awareness so that they can tell apart their emotions from those of others. Emotional empaths tend to withdraw from other people so that they can spend time alone and recharge. An emotional empath should protect their energy by following various healing practices.

- **Animal empaths**: You have certainly seen someone in your neighborhood who is more interested in keeping company with animals than human beings. They have a certain pet or even various pets that mean the world to them. There's a high likelihood that such a person is an animal empath. An animal empath feels a deep connection toward animals. They can sense what the animals want or feel, and the animals love them back. The connection is so deep that they have a way of communicating with each other. An animal empath answers to their intense desire of connecting with animals by domesticating their animals of choice. Also, they tend to be passionate about animal rights and make contributions to funds that advance animal welfare.

- **Plant empaths**: A plant empath shares a deep connection with a certain plant or plants in general. The plant evokes certain emotions when they touch it. A plant empath can communicate with the plant and can know its condition. They like hanging out near the plant in a natural environment, bringing it into their house, or planting it in the garden.

- **Precognitive empaths**: Are you the type of person that can always tell the future? And this is not down to your future alone, but also the future of other unrelated people or events? You're certainly a precognitive empath. You tend to "see" things before they actually come to pass. Your visions are made manifest in various ways such as dreams or feelings. Having this ability to foresee the future is both rewarding and distressing. It can help you brace for the future, and at the same time, it can amplify your misery knowing the pain that awaits you.
- **Psychometric empaths**: This sort of empath has a deep connection to various physical objects. The physical objects arouse certain emotions in them. The objects could range from utensils, knives, jewelry, photos, etc., but they each awaken certain deep emotions when the person comes across them. For instance, if your dad handed down his knife to you and then died that same day, the knife could have a lot of sentimental value. Every time you come across such a knife, you would miss your dad terribly.
- **Telepathic empath**: A telepathic empath can know what is stored away in someone's mind. With a casual glance at that person, they can tell their unexpressed thoughts. This causes the empath to have too much insight into people and situations.

CHAPTER 2: HOW TO RECOGNIZE IF YOU ARE AN EMPATH

An empath isn't defined by what they do, but what they are. If you're an empath, you were hard-wired to be that way since you were born, and you have an ultimate purpose in this. Most empaths don't realize that they can make a huge difference in the world by learning to let their special gift shine through and inspire others.

THE EMPATH IS LIKE THE COSMIC, EMOTIONAL CLEANER

Their gift can be used to both service themselves and those around them, helping humankind transform into something freer. When you are an empath you are highly affected not only by a peoples' communicated feelings but by their unconscious feelings and energies, as well. Whether a person is experiencing positive or negative feelings, thoughts, desires, motives, urges, or outward pressure, an empath is able to sense it. This sensing ability doesn't just mean that the empath is aware of these feelings, but they strongly feel them as if they were their own.

While we can learn to be more empathetic in daily life, working towards understanding another person's emotions and situation, you cannot learn to be an empath. Expressing empathy and being an empath are two totally different things. Empathy is something that most humans experience unless they have a mental disorder that affects the empathetic portion of the brain. Whereas being an empath is a natural trait that select people possess. You can gain an understanding of what empaths experience and why, but you can't make yourself into an empath no matter how much you try, it is not a learned ability.

In this chapter, we will explore some of the traits the empaths often portray along with a detailed list of ways to know whether or not you are an empath. By the end of this chapter, you will know the question of whether or not you are an empath. If you are an empath, then you will find help learning to use your ability within the remaining pages of this book. However, if you are not an empath you may still experience benefits in learning how to connect better with those around you and how to better understand the experiences empaths go through on a daily basis.

Do you regularly experience fatigue, confusion, distress, happiness, excitement, or even bodily pains simply from being around people? Sources of emotion and pain that don't appear to originate from inside your own mind or body, but from outside influences? When walking into a room with other people can you feel a deep sense of various emotions or thoughts? Empaths regularly express feeling this way, as they pick up on everyone's energy, emotions, motives, and sometimes even thoughts simply by being in near proximity to them. This can leave you feeling either drained or energized, depending upon the people you are interacting with and their emotions.

An empath may focus on the emotions rather than their own emotions and mental health needs. While neglecting their own needs an empath may decide to openly accept the emotions and thoughts of others. This is largely due to empaths seeking to improve the lives of others in a selfless manner. They are peacemakers who want to comfort those who are struggling, mend fences, and guide those in need. They can often do this in a gentle and non-aggressive manner, making them quite successful in helping others.

Although, while this can be born out a selfless desire, it may also be partly self-serving. By focusing on the experiences, emotions, and thoughts of other people an empath can ignore their own negative or difficult to accept feelings. By solving another person's problem and calming their emotions an empath may also lessen the number of negative emotions assaulting them on a daily basis. Some people may appreciate this help from the empath, but others may resent their involvement.

An empath, especially one who is not knowledgeable about their own abilities, is likely to adopt the feelings of others. As they do not understand where these feelings and emotions originated from, they often bottle it up and keep it inside themselves. As the empath does this their emotions become more volatile, gradually negatively affecting their mental and emotional well-being. An empath will find this affects them to an even larger degree if they have experienced previous mental trauma. The empath may find help and relief in talking out their emotions with a trusted person. This will allow the empath not only to receive empathy from another, but it will allow them to better understand their emotions as they speak.

Due to the overabundance of emotions that empaths experience some may become reclusive. While empaths can be both introverted and extroverted, one of these is not superior to the other. This is because both introverted and extroverted empaths may become reclusive, depending upon their personal experience and how the emotions negatively affect them. These empaths may learn to ignore and block out the emotions and energies of others, and in the process ignore their own feelings and struggles.

Yet, a healthy empath may become a force to be reckoned with. An empath may who knows how to use their ability can be well in-tune with their own emotions, as well as the emotions of those around them. While they may develop the ability to block out the emotions and energies of negative people, they aren't living life ignoring and burying these emotions. They can find a balance between experiencing emotions and blocking out negative emotions when needed. Because of this, an empath can use their ability to deepen their friendships, further their business, and overall improve their lives. A healthy and balanced empath often make people feel understood and connected, leaving them satisfied and better for having a conversation with the empath. Empaths are often found working in fields where they can help people and use their ability, such as when working with animals, people, or nature. They often use their energy to improve not only their lives but the world and those around them. Even if they are unable to get a job in their chosen field, they may volunteer their time in order to benefit society.

Many empaths have deep and vivid imaginations, which enables them to become marvelous creators, artists, and storytellers. This can sometimes make them more romantic, making them want to see the good and fascinating aspects of life. They may become an artist in multiple ways, whether with a paintbrush, a keyboard, or a whisk in the kitchen. This may also result in the empath having a strong tie to their past and ancestors. The empath sees the importance of their heritage and seeks to find a deeper connection with it, possibly becoming a family historian.

If you are an empath you may find that you experience a deep connection to music and its various elements. Lyrics within a song may have an especially profound effect on an empath, as they deeply feel the emotions communicated. But if an empath if overwhelmed with emotion then music may add to the sense of burden. In these cases, an empath should avoid lyrical music and stick to pure musical pieces that calm their mind.

Just as empaths are prone to be affected by music, they can be greatly affected by other media around them. The news and current events can become especially overwhelming, as the empath desired to help and is left unable to do this in many situations. By seeing news stories of pain or abuse experienced by other humans or animals an empath may become unable to manage their emotions or day, becoming depressed and isolated. While empaths may be able to understand emotions to a wide extent, in these situations they struggle with understanding how other people can be so cruel and lacking in compassion. This may lead empaths to be highly selective in the news or books they read and the television they watch.

Both people and animals are often drawn to empaths as if they were a magnet. The empath's genuine kindness, concern, compassion, and openness can attract people from all walks of life. They can see that the empath is accepting and unlikely to cause friction or drama. Even someone who is a complete stranger can find it easy to speak with an empath about their life, emotions, and personal matters. Before long the person realizes that they have shared their life story and poured their heart out to the empath, without consciously realizing it. This is because empaths are naturally easy to talk to and the person feels the deep connection with them. Empaths often feel satisfied and fulfilled by these conversations. However, it is important that the empath isn't always the one listening, but that they have an opportunity to talk and express themselves. If an empath is abandoned during moments of high emotion it can greatly affect them in a negative way. While the empath frequently expresses love, caring, and kindness, if they are deprived of this themselves, they will have difficulty recovering.

Along with verbally expressing emotions, empaths frequently express their feelings and thoughts with body language and creativity. They may be drawn to dancing, acting, or other expressive movements. During this time an empath may get lost in the feelings they are expressing or music that is playing. They can project an incredible sense of emotion and energy that unconsciously affects those around them.

Many empaths are dreamers. They focus on more than the here and now and the mundane. If life becomes uninteresting or boring it is not uncommon for the empath to become detached from reality and absorb themselves in a daydream. This may also manifest in vivid or lucid dreams during sleep. Not only does this mean that they dream in great detail, but empaths are likely to be curious about their dreams, their contents, and their meaning. Empaths are likely to see meaning in dreams, rather than seeing them as irrelevant nonsense.

Along with seeking meaning within their dreams, empaths are likely to search for the meaning throughout many aspects of life. They are often inquisitive thinkers who are willing to study and solve problems and questions. An empath will search for answers in order to gain peace of mind, whether it is at school, home, work, or in their social life. Due to their empathetic ability, they will more easily be able to intuitively learn and pick up knowledge, understanding the meaning behind the words spoken.

Throughout their lives, many empaths are told that they are simply overly sensitive. They don't understand their emotions and what is going on within them, leading to an overabundance of emotions. They may cry a lot, not knowing what else to do with the sense of confusion. While they know they are experiencing an abundance of emotions, they are unaware of where they originate from. This can be especially confounding as one minute they were fine and the next they were assaulted with unknown emotions. They can feel happy and energized, and then the next moment depressed and lethargic. These empaths need to understand their ability and the ways it impacts them personally and the world outside them in order to fully flourish and feel comfortable with themselves.

If you are an empath, then you have an amazing gift. You are intuitive and have the unique ability of understanding and connecting with others on a deeper level than most. You don't have to rely on long conversations in order to understand someone's feelings or intent. Along with feeling their emotions on a mental and emotional level, you may even be able to experience it on a physical level. If this sounds like you, then you may just be an empath. Following is a list of the most common traits in empaths. If you find yourself matching most of these then it is safe to say that you are in fact an empath.

Adopting the emotions of those around you. Empaths adopt the emotions of those around them as if they were their own. Sometimes this is only when a person is in close proximity to them, but other times the person may be a great distance away. The exact range will depend upon the individual empath.

Simply knowing things without being told. Empaths can become attuned into other people to an extent that you can glean knowledge simply by being around them. This is much more profound than simply having a gut feeling or being intuitive.

Having the ability to discern truth from deception. Empaths have a distinct ability to know when a friend or loved one is lying to them. Although, some empaths may be able to pick up even when complete strangers are lying to them.

Empaths may have the ability to develop mimicking physical symptoms from other people. They frequently will pick up symptoms such as body paints, viruses, and infections as a form of sympathy pain.

Many empaths have a strong need for solitude. Due to feeling the emotions of those around them, it's important for an empath to have some alone time where they can decompress. This is especially true for empathic children.

Nature and animals can play an incredible role in the lives of many empaths. By spending time outdoors or with animals they have the ability to recharge and destress.

The creative arts are a common past time for empaths. Whether it is painting, singing, baking, acting, molding clay, or dancing.

Empaths may easily become bored, which is especially true if they don't have any attention-grabbing stimulation. This may make work and school difficult if they are unable to doodle or daydream.

Many people will tell their problems to an empath, even if they are a complete stranger. If the empath isn't careful, then they may become everyone's go-to source when troubled or worried until they are overwhelmed.

Empaths may be prone to mood swings, due to the wide range of emotions affecting them. When overtaxed they may appear disconnected, shy, or aloof. This makes them miserable and they must deal with the overabundance of emotions in order to better cope.

It is nearly unbearable for empaths to watch violence or cruelty depicted on television. This is especially true when the violence or cruelty depicted is reality rather than fiction, such as with the news or historical documentaries.

Crowded public areas, such as stadiums, concerts, shopping malls, bars, parties, and grocery stories frequently overwhelm empaths. These environments are filled with the emotions of other people, constantly assaulting the empath.

Frequently looking out for the underdog. Empaths often look out for those who may be struggling through a difficult time in a variety of ways. They hope to help comfort these people and protect them from further harm.

Those who are empaths are more likely to struggle with an addictive personality. This includes addiction in many areas, such as drugs, alcohol, gambling, sex, and more. Empaths may use these to cope with the onslaught of emotions and must be aware that they may easily develop one of these, or a number of other, addictions.

Empaths are seekers of truth, frequently searching for a truthful answer to any of their questions. It can be incredibly frustrating for an empath to have unanswered questions. Therefore, if they have questions they will research and look for the truth.

When an empath doesn't enjoy something, they struggle with completing it. They are unable to focus and feel deep unhappiness whenever doing something they don't enjoy. This effect is compounded upon if they are being forced into doing something with guilt or manipulation.

Empaths are frequently free spirits who love adventure, travel, and to be free.

An empath has a supreme listening ability, able to fully immerse themselves in what a person is saying to them. Yet, they are unlikely to talk as much about themselves unless it is with someone that they trust.

A strict routine, schedule, control, or rules feels as if it's imprisonment for empaths. If anything takes away their freedom, then they will fight back.

Empaths are incredibly tolerant and forgiving of other people. But they are unable to tolerate being around narcissistic people. As empaths are so attuned to the emotions of those around them it is unjustifiable to them that others may discard the feelings of others while being egotistical.

An empath may struggle with fatigue more than a healthy person. This is due to the large amount of energy affecting them from other people. They become drained and tired, unable to process more emotions without rest. Empaths are often drawn to fields of healing, although they may not be able to manage in the field as they are so profoundly affected by their emotions that they are unable to maintain a professional distance.

Lastly, empaths are frequently drawn to spirituality, metaphysics, the paranormal, and the otherwise unexplained.

By now you have a strong idea of whether or not you are an empath. If you are, congratulations! You are reading a book that will help you use your natural ability in a way that is fulfilling and beneficial. If you aren't an empath you may still benefit from this book by learning how people you know may be empaths.

CHAPTER 3: EMPATH AND HIGHLY SENSITIVE PEOPLE

Highly sensitive persons are those who have a condition where the nervous system processes more input than usual. HSPs can be born with it but some develop it sometime during their life.

Empaths are highly attuned to emotions – their own and that of other humans. Some empaths can sense the emotions of animals and plants. Like HSPs, empaths are born being able to do what they can, but others have learned to be more sensitive to feelings as they grew up.

HSPs and empaths are often considered to be the same condition because they have similar traits, but this is a misconception. The most important difference between them is that HSPs are sensitive to what their five senses can perceive while empaths have extra-sensory perception. In other words, empaths are psychics while HSPs are not necessarily psychics.

There are more HSPs than empaths. It has been estimated that 15-20% of the population are HSPs and only 3% are empaths. Many empaths are also HSPs but only few HSPs are empaths. One of these conditions does not necessarily lead to another.

What HSPs and empaths have in common is they are both highly sensitive. They naturally process more input than what others do. This makes them notice more things and think/feel more deeply about them.

LIVING LIFE WITH HIGH SENSITIVITY

If you are an HSP, empath, or both, you may notice that you're different from others. Because of your traits, you are more perceptive than usual. This enables you to understand more and process information more thoroughly than the average person. On the downside, this can make you overload easily. You may struggle with things that others don't even notice.

Having high sensitivity has its advantages in social life. You can connect to people at deeper levels. You are aware of what another person is really feeling even if he/she tries to hide it. You understand people's motivations, so you know what to expect from them. This insight is quite helpful if you work with people a lot in your chosen field of work; this is the case if you are a manager, psychologist, counselor, teacher, coach, salesperson, therapist, nurse, investigator, lawyer, etc.

You have the potential to solve problems and improve relationships because you can take on various perspectives. You comprehend the dynamics of relationships and situations, so you know why people and things became how they are now. Noticing more gives you insights that help you communicate more effectively. This can increase your credibility and influence – in fact, many advisors are highly sensitive.

The downside is that you may have problems handling situations and tasks that need objectivity. Being sensitive to others' feelings, you may find it hard to make decisions that affect others negatively. This may cause you to become indecisive or stressed when you have to do something that isn't exactly positive for someone else—such as laying people off for not being productive.

Your highly sensitive nervous system may cause you to be more anxious in social situations as well. You may be prone to strong emotions and frequent mood swings, especially if you are an empath on top of being an HSP.

Fortunately, the drawbacks of high sensitivity can be managed by learning how to manage stimuli and practicing how to respond to it. Just like with other people, an HSP/empath can learn how to be better in social life with constant practice.

Overall, high sensitivity is simply a trait that is neither good nor bad. It just depends on what you do with it. The next chapter is about dealing with toxic relationships. Knowing how to handle energy vampires and difficult people can make social life more productive and less tiresome.

CHAPTER 4: UNDERSTANDING THE POTENTIALS OF YOUR ENERGY AND ABILITIES

Empaths have a better understanding of energy than they do the words that are coming out of a person's mouth. This is one of the reasons you can't lie to an empath—they will sense it. Empaths can listen to someone speaking a language they don't understand but have full insight into what they are trying to express based on their energy. Empaths listen to words, pay attention to body language, and translate energetic vibrations. They are especially vulnerable to negativity because it takes from their energy field. On the other hand, when empaths are surrounded by positive energy, they become relaxed and their aura expands in an outward direction as their feelings and emotions flow freely without tension. Positive energy is like a charger—it boosts you up and refills you.

This is why empaths will avoid conflict at all costs, shut down when confronted with it, and stay away from certain people and places. The body goes into self-defense mode in an attempt to preserve energy so that you don't become tired and exhausted. Whether you know it or not, empaths can choose who and what influences their energy—they decide where it is sent and to whom. Our thoughts are so powerful that as soon as they are released, anyone capable of tuning in to your frequency will automatically pick them up. In other words, empaths have the ability to read minds. A skilled empath knows how to protect themselves by being fully aware of what is taking place around them and being present so that no one is able to enter their energy field without their permission.

Once you learn how energy works, it is important that you use it wisely. Remember what goes around comes around, and whatever you put out into the world will come right back to you. Energy is like a drug—the more you experiment with it and enjoy the way it makes you feel, the easier it is to become addicted to it. Your energy, if not protected, will abandon you, become reckless, and attach itself to any other energy circulating in the atmosphere. When empaths are alert and aware, they can quickly recognize subtle changes that take place in their environment without needing to use any of their five senses—smell, touch, taste, sight, or hearing. Once energy has been released, it travels in an outward direction and never dies. It remains in the air and clings to people or objects, and other energies absorb it or connect with it. Our energy leaves a legacy wherever we go, which is why you can step into an environment and immediately pick up on the vibe of it. That vibe is dependent upon the people or the event that is taking place there. Once you realize that your energy is constantly interacting with other people's energy, regardless of space, time, or distance, it can become overwhelming, and you will feel as though you need to get back to yourself. But this is because society has conditioned us to believe that our mind and body are two separate entities.

Empaths have a deep desire to discover who they are and what they were put on this earth to do. The awakening process is an extremely traumatic and painful one, parallel to the metamorphosis of the caterpillar into a butterfly. It is a dark and lonely time, but once you discover your truth, you will emerge like a beautiful butterfly and soar to new heights. It is during this time that you come to the revelation that we are not separate or individual but a part of something tremendous—energy and the universe.

You are not always going to be able to explain your gift because there are some aspects of it that are illogical, and in a world that relies on logic, mathematics, and scientific studies, this can be difficult to comprehend. Empaths feel and sense their way through life. They do not need men in white coats to explain what they inherently know about their natural existence. People who don't understand the gift will chalk it up to whatever their imaginations can conjure up and refuse to believe that such a thing exists. Such people are afraid to challenge the status quo and think outside the box; they are afraid of the unknown. They are confined by what they can see with their natural eyes, and if they can't see it, they won't believe it.

Once you have extensive knowledge of how energy works, you will immediately discover limitless mind-blowing possibilities. You will realize that your energy never dies and in whatever form it takes, it will continue to exist. When your life is determined by time, you can become disillusioned, especially if you have reached a certain age and not achieved all that you had hoped. When you were 16, you had envisioned that you would be married with kids by the age of 30. But by the age of

35, you still haven't found your soul mate and so you start worrying about how much time you have left to fulfill your dreams. You realize that you have wasted your time slaving away in a job that you don't like, or that you have married the wrong person and allowed your soulmate to slip through your fingers. In reality, time doesn't exist. The universe has no regard for it. Man created time, and we have structured our lives around it. If time was abolished, there would be mayhem because people wouldn't know what to do with themselves. When we get to a certain age and our bodies start to decay, we assume that time is running out. But even when our bodies have returned to dust, our energy will continue to travel throughout the universe—there is no beginning and no end. We existed before we took residence on earth in a human body, and we will continue to exist when this body disintegrates.

Physically and mentally, empaths are different. Our bodies are porous, so they absorb energy into their muscles, organs, and tissues. This means that you feel other people's pain, distress, suffering, and depression. You can feel every negative emotion even though they don't belong to you, which can have a detrimental effect on your health. On the other hand, you can quickly get in tune with other people's love, happiness, and vitality, which is a fantastic feeling. Empaths feel exhausted when they are surrounded by toxic people, witnessing arguments, violence, and hearing too much noise makes empaths feel physically ill.

Empaths can also feel other people's physical pain and pick up the same symptoms as if they had the illness. This is one of the reasons they find it difficult to work in hospitals. You might find that your mood changes when you get on a bus and sit next to someone who is depressed or anxious. Or you can walk into a store feeling happy or even neutral, but leave feeling tense and exhausted, or even with aches and pains in your body because you have been exposed to the whirlwind of chaos that usually takes place in a store with the bright lights, loud speakers, and crowds of people. There are certain environments that are simply not conducive for empaths.

To survive as an empath, it's crucial to learn how to ground yourself in overstimulating situations and protect yourself against other people's negative energy.

CHAPTER 5: COPING WITH SPIRITUAL HYPERSENSITIVITY

As a highly sensitive person, you will often come into contact with people who are hard to deal with. The following are tips on how to handle such people:

ALWAYS KEEP YOUR COOL

It can be so tempting to lash out when you encounter someone who is not being reasonable. But don't fall into that temptation. The moment you lash out, you lose your power and make the aggressor look big. You should maintain your cool so that you can be in control of the conversation. For instance, if a client proves to be hard to work with, don't yell at them; instead, stay calm and work out a solution. Yelling at people will only trigger them as they fight for their egos. It takes incredible maturity to maintain your calm when someone is obviously looking for a fight. However, in such instances, you should deflect their efforts and, if possible, ask for the intervention of a bigger influence. Aggressors tend to be confounded when their tricks don't seem to excite the reaction they intended.

MIND YOUR OWN BUSINESS

You cannot save the world. Some people are purposely difficult as though they want to see who is triggered by their actions. If you realize that someone has a tendency of wanting to test the patience of other people, you should not give them the satisfaction of falling into their trap. Look the other way and continue minding your business. When they realize that you have no interest in their games, they will drop their act. Always mind your business so that you don't get into much trouble in the first place.

SET BOUNDARIES

Boundaries are guidelines that you set for other people expressing the permissible way they can behave toward you, and how you will react if the boundaries are crossed. For instance, if you experience friction at work, you may tell your coworkers that you don't appreciate being disturbed once you start working. When you retreat to your desk, they should stay away and wait to engage you once you're free. Having boundaries helps you manage how other people will behave toward you. You should spell out clear terms regarding your boundaries, and if someone trespasses, make sure to mete out punishment.

LEARN TO SEE THE BIGGER PICTURE

Sometimes we are so vested in our own interests that we fail to see the big picture. This attitude tends to promote conflict instead of eliminating conflict. For instance, if you think that your parents are not being reasonable, you can potentially raise hell. In as much as you might think that your parents only want to make your life miserable, think of what they want you to have in the future. If you see their grand plans, it is easy to appreciate what they are doing for you at present.

CHOOSE YOUR BATTLES WISELY

You need to choose your battles wisely. There are some battles that you stand no chance of winning – and you know it. For instance, if you work for an impossible boss, it can be so tempting to try to fight them. But think of the power that your boss wields. They can terminate you from work. And then you have nowhere to fight from. Always pick the battles that you know you stand a chance of winning. This will save you much heartache and also boost your winning streak.

SEPARATE THE PERSON FROM THE ISSUE

It is so easy to fall into the trap of thinking that another person holds a personal grudge against you. However, when you take things personally, you lose the ability to be objective. Always learn to separate the problem from the person. This will allow you to have a fresh perspective on matters. When you take things personally, you can hardly make any progress – since you will only be interested in taking vengeance. Being objective is critical. It will help you articulate the issue you have with another person and how to solve the problem.

HAVE A SENSE OF HUMOR

The secret to overcoming your hurdles is to meet them with a sense of humor. For instance, if your life partner makes a decision that hurts you, don't recoil away in horror and start calculating how to hurt them back. Instead, reach out to your sense of humor and see the fun side of what your partner has done. Having a sense of humor will help you pull through life's challenges by increasing your creativity. It allows you to have a new perspective on your circumstances.

ASK FOR HELP

What would you do if a 3oo-pound man hurt you? Obviously, you wouldn't attempt to fight back if you're physically weak. But you might press charges against that person. There are systems and people in place to help you get even with the people who have wronged you. Utilize these systems instead of taking matters into your own hands. If your life partner has wronged you, there's no need of becoming violent; just report them to the relevant authorities. Whenever you find yourself pitted against someone who's unreasonable, instead of going through more pain, reach out to someone who can assist you.

BECOME EXPERIENCED

There are two ways of viewing your troubles – as a punishment or as a learning experience. If you consider your trouble to be a punishment, you have a victim mentality, and you won't become a better person. However, if you view your trouble as an opportunity to learn, you will become experienced at spotting patterns that lead to trouble with others. The more experienced you are at handling different types of people; the fewer problems you will have considering that you know how to handle various types. Whenever you are in a tight situation, and someone is giving you a difficult time of it, try to learn their pattern.

Stress is a natural part of life. This is the body's mechanism for dealing with the problems we face on a daily basis. No one can say they have not ever felt stressed. Generally, all stress is bad. But your stress can be considered good if it turns out to be beneficial to you. Stress is good if it causes you to focus more, gets you motivated, and challenges you specially to meet your goals. There are some people who have an abundance of stress. The empath is one such person with a high definition stress factor.

As an empath, you have the ability to draw emotions from around you.

EMPATHS NATURALLY STRUGGLE WITH THE FOLLOWING SITUATIONS

- **Anxiety** – Empaths become especially anxious in unfamiliar situations, whether it is a place, an occasion or event. You can be feeling new energies and not able to determine where they are coming from.
- It is also easy for you to pull anxiety from those around you. You cannot do anything about it, which causes you to feel more anxious.
- **Burden** – As you draw different emotions from around you, there is the tendency to carry around their weight. They can be very burdensome. Picture an animal forced to carry weights all the time.
- The difference? You were not made to haul burdens; therefore, you feel deep sadness all the time. And, your melancholy interferes with your normal daily tasks.
- **Illness** – When you are so stressed with overwhelming, unexplained anxiety, the body goes into overdrive and you feel sick. You are more liable than the ordinary person to have heart palpitations, headaches, sleeplessness, and to experience nightmares. Identify stressful situations overwhelming you; find ways to handle them. You may not be able to shake your stress permanently. But you need to learn to manage it so it does not overrun you. Explore the following techniques and use them to help you manage your stress.

Emotional Freedom Technique (EFT) is one of the newer methods being used to handle stress. This technique taps certain acupressure points of the body.

One of the major benefits of EFT is it can be useful in removing negative emotions. It uses the same meridian points as acupuncture to treat emotional and physical illnesses. EFT is based on tapping several meridian points with the tip of the fingers while repeating positive affirmations.

Here is how EFT works.

- **Step 1** - Identify a problem causing you stress. It may be something about which you are frustrated or angry.
- **Step 2** - Find the meridian points to use. Locate them on the different parts of the upper body.
    - **On the head** - One point is located on the top of the head.
    - **On the Face** - There are the bones right beside the eyes. Some experts use those areas on the inner part of the eyes where the brows seem to meet. Farther down the face are the bones immediately under the eyes and the areas under the nose and lips.
    - **On your Hand** - You will use the karate chop points on the soft part of your hands. The inner parts of both your wrists are important, too.
    - **On the Torso** - Feel the areas just under the two collarbones. Lastly, touch the area about three inches below the armpits.
- **Step 3** – Start tapping beside your eyes using the tips of your three middle fingers. Remember to use the soft parts of the fingertips.
- **Step 4** – As you tap, concentrate on the situation bothering you.
- **Step 5** – Repeat a statement of affirmation such as, "Although I am anxious, I deeply and completely accept myself." Do this as many times as required until the problem has receded into nothingness.

You can perform the technique at any time during the day, but preferably at night before going to sleep

GROUNDING AND COPING TECHNIQUES FOR EMPATHIC ABILITIES

UNDERSTANDING YOUR EMPATH ABILITIES

If you understand your empathic abilities, you are on your way to becoming an empowered empath. You will have to discover ways to cope with the strange emotions you carry. Finding yourself with strong, perceptible emotions can be scary and very overwhelming. You possibly have gone to a few public places and found you feel like exploding emotionally. You ask yourself, "Why do I feel so sad?" "Where did this anger come from all of a sudden?"

Furthermore, there is so much tension and turmoil going on inside of you, all you want to do is go home, lock the door behind you, turn off the light, and crawl under the covers. You really want to get some relief in your mind. At the same time, you find you have great power to give, to love, to care, and to exhibit compassion. You are extremely happy when you are helping people.

Like many other empaths, you may not have the slightest idea what is going on with you. You may have tried to shake the feeling. Or to put a spin on it. You may pass it off as being different and rationalize it will go away in a while. Be mindful, your empath abilities are with you to stay. You may even consider yourself a little crazy - friends, families and strangers are thinking the same way, too.

But you have only come into your own because you have discovered and accepted your abilities are a gift. Understand - you need to own and to use it your gift to heal others. Respond positively to the negative energies instead of fighting them so you can live a more empowered and happier life. In order to understand all that is taking place with you, embrace the emotions and consider them useful tools.

See them as your guiding force, something you can use to chart a good path. They will be your best friends and you'll want to call upon for the rest of your life.

BECOME AWARE OF YOUR FEELING

One of the ways to handle your feeling is to become aware of what is happening to you. Try to determine if the emotion you are experiencing in a particular moment is yours or someone else's. If, for example, during a pleasant and peaceful day, you suddenly get irritable and sad, find out if it is your feeling or if another source is influencing you.

What about your intense headache?

From where did it emerge, considering you are not prone to headaches? Look at who is around you.

With whom did you talk recently?

What was the conversation about?

Could the source of your stress be yours?

Ask a lot of questions in order to root out the cause. Once you discover the source, you can extricate yourself. Consider also, you can experience an emotional shift even if you are not around someone. Yes, you can draw from another person's energy even telepathically. When this is happening, you tend to think you are the problem. Being an "aware empath" will help you to handle your sensitivities and bring the right perspective about who you are. You are going to keep what is yours and apply the appropriate treatment to anything coming from a different source.

NOTICE SIGNS OF OVERSENSITIVITY

Another way to cope with your empathic stress is to identify your oversensitivity.

There are certain traits you have, and these include being a highly sensitive person.

- **You can tell how a person is feeling.** You are not just having a moment of intuition as we would normally say or think. It is more. You have picked up strong emotions from people around you. The person does not have to be in close proximity to you either. Your sensitivity can be telepathic.

- **People tell you are too emotional.** You cry a lot when you see someone or something (such as an animal) is suffering. You cannot stand watching certain shows on TV because they are very painful for you.
- **You are very sensitive to the issues of others.** Many people are drawn to you because of your caring nature. You are able to listen people's problems for hours on end.
- **You ignore your own needs.** You are always looking after the needs of others. It is as natural to you as eating.
- **You alternate between moods.** One minute you are happy and loving; the next, you are "on the other side of the wall" –cranky and difficult. This occurs because, as you shift between environments, you pick up on different emotions. You have entered energy overload and you go where the tide leads.

RIDDING YOURSELF OF EXCESS ENERGY

Now that you can tap into your awareness and determine the sources of your stress, you need to find ways of dealing with them. You will already know the feelings can be overwhelming. Consider what happens when you keep pulling energies from people all around you, and not able to relieve yourself of them. You are a prime target for energy overload. You are like a ticking time bomb. The more that is piled on you, the greater your chance to disintegrate. You do not need to remain so "loaded". Let's look at some ways to deal with excess energy.

1. GROUND YOURSELF

To ground yourself is to realize the Earth's powerful healing attributes and use it to release excess energy. Diane Katherine refers to it as "Earthing".

There are a host of benefits derived from groundings.

- It reduces empaths fatigue. You can become extremely exhausted from encounters with different energies invading your energy field.

- Using electronics such as television, phone, and computer can disrupt the bioelectrical system of your body. There is the potential for your energy field to be left open, making it easier for other energies to invade.
- You can use groundings to clear energies you have drawn from others.
- Groundings helps you take control of all the chaotic thoughts and make you keep only positive and healthy thoughts.
- Ultimately, you will have a stronger energy field giving greater protection from the external energy forces creeping in unawares.
- You will experience calm and, ultimately, less stress.
- One of the most basic techniques involving grounding is to connect with the ground.
- Simply remove your shoes and stand barefooted.
- Press your feet into the ground and experience the natural feel and coolness of the Earth.
- Close your eyes and release your energy and all your emotions into the Earth.
- Thank the Earth for taking your negative energies and give the assurance you will not allow them to affect you again.
- Imagine a beautiful golden light on the top of your head – the crown chakra. Let this beautiful light enter and light up your whole being. Let it run right down to your root chakra. Allow the light to replace any excess energy remaining in you. Let the light also flow outside and surround you. It will become a protective barrier prohibiting any negative energies from coming back inside of you.
- Allow the light to go when you have felt the release.

2. DO CLEARINGS

Clear your excess energies, especially the negative and unhealthy ones. Take advantage of the following technique.

- Close your eyes.
- Bring your thoughts to your heart's center and let them rest there.
- Imagine there is a ball of light in your heart's center.
- Take the ball and burst it outward, releasing all its contents.

- As you do so, speak to your action, saying, "I release all energies that do not belong to me".

3. PRACTICE ZIPPING UP

Imagine an energy line (or path) running down the center of your torso. Energies can enter this pathway through the crown of your head and invade all your system. To utilize the zip-up technique, mimic the gesture of zipping the pathway closed. How do you do it?

- Place your hand (you can use both hands) just above your pubic bones. Let your palms face you.
- Breathing deeply and slowly, move your hand up your torso and up to your lips. Note! You can let your hand move against your body or a few inches from it.
- Image you are closing the zipper.

CHAPTER 7: PROTECT YOURSELF FROM NARCISSISTS AND OTHER ENERGY VAMPIRES

Have you ever gone somewhere feeling vibrant and after spending time around that place, you felt drained of energy? Or have you ever met someone and after spending time with them, you felt an energy drain? Both of these situations point to an encounter with an energy vampire. Most energy vampires are only interested in their own desires, lack empathy, and are incredibly immature. An energy vampire will leave you feeling exhausted, irritated, and overwhelmed. An energy vampire can be anyone – friends, family, coworkers, etc. Once you realize that someone is a vampire, you should do yourself a favor and cut them off from your life. Getting rid of an energy vampire is not a self-serving deed; it is an act of self-preservation. The vibrations of energy, vampires are incredibly low. As a coping strategy, they have to suck energy from others through the following ways:

- **Gossiping** - An energy vampire knows that people want to hear a good story. So, they say anything in an attempt to earn the attention of their victim. They resort to telling lies about people. If an energy vampire tells you about other people, you can be sure that they will tell other people about you as well. They also start slow wars between factions by telling each side antagonizing news.
- **Manipulation** - An energy vampire is a master manipulator. Before they approach anyone, they already have a script to play by and have rehearsed how to take advantage of that person. They have no remorse about manipulating people into doing their bidding, as their capacity to empathize is incredibly limited. Energy vampires get a high out of manipulating people and getting their way.
- **Complaining** - No one is more "wronged" in the entire world. An energy vampire believes that the world is out to get them. They can take advantage of someone and yet find a way of twisting the story so that they appear to be the victims. An energy vampire is good at weaving stories together, and they have the experience of passing themselves off as victims. Due to this habit of complaining, an energy vampire tends to be slack in their work, knowing too well they can find something to complain about or someone to throw the blame at.

- **Massive ego** - An energy vampire has a massive ego, and it comes with delusions of grandeur. An energy vampire sets themselves extremely ambitious goals. The goals are unrealistic because they lack the wherewithal of achieving these goals. Their massive ego also manifests in how they treat other people. Energy vampires think that they are special people and are above everyone else. Thus, they act self-entitled and expect everyone to bow down to them. When an energy vampire comes into your life, they will normally have an agenda of taking something away from you, before they move on to the next victim.
- **Not being accountable** - An energy vampire will hardly ever be accountable for anything. They want easy things and hate responsibility. Due to this hatred of accountability, energy vampires make the worst candidates for doing any serious task. They will usually disappoint you. If you have to rely on an energy vampire for the completion of a task, they will frustrate you with their subpar performance and an unwillingness to be accountable. Energy vampires will develop a hatred toward anyone that expects them to be answerable, but when the shoe is on the other foot, they are extremely ruthless.
- **Neglecting the needs of their dependents** - Energy vampires are only interested in their own needs and woe unto anyone that depends on them. For instance, if the energy vampire in question has a family, they may spend their earnings on vain things like sex and alcohol at the expense of their family. The people that depend on an energy vampire lead very sad lives because of both the cruelty and humiliation that the energy vampire metes out at them. More often than not, children raised by energy vampires turn into social misfits because they have known nothing but pain their whole lives.
- When an energy vampire is around you, you will feel uneasy, and soon your energy levels will take a massive dip. The following are some things that take place when attacked by an energy vampire:
- **Nausea** - After an interaction with an energy vampire, you can be left feeling nauseous. This feeling may be accompanied by a stomachache. This happens because your body is going through a lot of stress because of losing energy. Once you get rid of the energy vampire, both the nausea and the stomachache will go away.

- **Headache** - An energy vampire will also make you experience a terrible headache. Once your energy levels go down, there's not enough energy for your brain. The brain reacts by trying to create awareness of the fact that the body has run out of sugars. The brain consumes a significant portion of the total energy of a person, and if the energy suffers a drop, a person's ability to use their mental faculties is severely affected. Once you find out that someone is an energy vampire, the ultimate remedy is to cut the person out of your life. However, in some instances, you're stuck with them because they play an indispensable role in your life. The following are tips to help you cope against attacks from energy vampires:
- **Set boundaries** - Let the person know that you have boundaries that are not to be crossed. This limits the time that you get to spend around the energy vampire.
- **Recite positive mantras** - Mantras are short phrases that a person says over and over with the intention of reaffirming a particular belief. Create more positive energy for yourself by reciting mantras.
- **Visualization** - Using your mind's eye, visualize a membrane of light around your body, shielding your energy from loss. This will greatly reduce the amount of energy lost to the vampire.

CHAPTER 8: GET INTO INTIMATE RELATIONSHIPS

The ability to communicate effectively with your partner is one that you build over time. The strength of your bond determines the quality of your communication. This, in turn, determines its longevity. Relationships have never been as fickle as they are today. Separation and divorce cases have become so common, it is no longer news. It is not unusual to see a couple in its 20s already divorced. What is it that we're doing wrong? We have several older couples that have been together for decades, and back then it was the norm. We need to put in conscious effort into our relationships. Healthy relationships translate into a healthy society. We definitely need to do better.

LOVE YOURSELF

This already sounds like a cliché statement, right? You must have heard it so many times before. Either way, it does not lose its validity. A relationship is not a combination of 2 halves. It is the bringing together of 2 whole people to complement each other. Your partner is not there to complete you. You're already whole. Or at least you should be.

Create a life for yourself. Have a job, business, hobby, friends or any other thing that fascinates you. Attend to your interests. Treat your body and mind. Many relationships are failing because people are over-relying on their partners. It is not the duty of your partner to make you happy. If you have not managed to find happiness in all those years, don't you think it's a huge task to place on someone else? Create the life that you want, then invite your partner to share in the joy.

BE HONEST

Lies destroy a lot of relationships. Can you be trusted by your partner? Can he or she trust you to do exactly as you agreed? Can you remain faithful in your relationship? What is the worst that your partner can do if you actually told the truth? They say that lies have a very short life span. Here's another one: there are 3 things that you cannot hide; the sun, the moon, and the truth. Sooner or later, the truth comes out. The liar may try to tell another lie to cover up for the first one. Why go through so much trouble?

Lies then breed mistrust. You begin to doubt every word that comes out of your partner's mouth. When trust is broken, things are never the same. They say that broken trust is like a broken vase. You can glue it back together, but it will never be the same again. Cultivate a culture of honesty where you tell things as they are, even when they're bad. Avoid overreacting in anger when you're told the truth. Take time to calm down then you can talk it over. Such an approach will encourage your partner to tell the truth.

CONNECT

We're often preoccupied with the developments of our lives that we forget to make time for our significant other. Granted, those bills will not pay themselves. But there has to be a limit. You may be out there hell-bent on chasing the dollar to give your family a better life, but by the time you get your money together, you have no family to speak of. Make it a priority to bond with your partner. Set aside time and observe it as strictly as you observe your work schedule. Spend quality time without your phones or any other distractions.

Get to know how each other is doing beyond the surface. You may be assuming that your partner is fine just because he/she is going on with life as normal, but that could be far from it. Discuss deeper matters; mental health, job satisfaction, inner battles, goals, dreams and so on. Go for the holidays. Go for dates. Visit places that are significant to your relationship. Go clubbing and dancing, just as you did when you were younger. That will add a breath of fresh air to your relationship.

EMPATHY

In the world acclaimed relationship book **Men are from Mars; Women from Venus**, the author John gray expounds that men and women have very different needs. They view the world differently. Men have a hard time understanding why a woman would be so bothered by some dress at the store not fitting. They will even argue with the attendant when told to try one a size bigger. Matters of weight are close to their hearts. They often ask all legendary 'do I look fat in these?' Can you empathize with your wife in that situation? Similarly, women hardly understand why men mourn when a team loses. You'd think somebody died!

Here both parties will have their empathy tested. Empathy involves stepping into the shoes of your partner so you can feel their emotions and see things from their point of view. In this case, the husband can suggest that the wife joins a fitness club so that the dress will eventually fit. The wife can, in turn, sympathize with the guy on his loss, and perhaps cook him his favorite meal to make him feel better. It sounds like a good idea, right?

PRODUCTIVE CONFLICT

Disagreements can make or break your relationship. In most cases, they break. But you can handle them such that they even leave your bond stronger. Agree to set aside some conflict time and place. Even if you're dealing with an issue, don't result in a shouting match all over the house. Sometimes the verbal wall even goes beyond your house. Set aside a time when you're both relaxed. Let's say a Saturday afternoon. Set the place as well. Perhaps in the study room or in the backyard, since the outdoors makes everything better. There you can outline all your issues, discuss them and find the way forward. This does not mean that you will always agree. But you can agree to disagree. You can choose to respect each other's opinions even when you don't agree with it.

SPEND TIME ALONE

The quality of your relationship is determined by the status of the 2 of you. If either of you is fatigued, stressed, disgruntled, dissatisfied or depressed, it will end up affecting both of you. It is a good idea to take time alone to refresh. Go do the things that make you happy. Go shop for new clothes. Get a haircut, a massage or a spa treatment. You can even take a brief holiday. Take this moment to rejuvenate, heal and reflect. By the time you go back to your partner, you will be a refreshed person, and it will mirror your relationship. These tips should help you strengthen your relationship, so you can go through the ups and downs of life together. With such a bond, your communication will be so much better.

Intentional change always begins with awareness. The empath's world can be boggling, and life becomes much less so when the conditions are understood. Children sometimes become upset when unable to describe what is happening on the inside. Once they have words to convey their agitation, however, they quickly calm down, because what was once vague is now real. Empaths live in a world they often can't describe. They doubt its validity, as well as their perceptions. Sensitives benefit greatly from observation and understanding why they have been feeling what they have been feeling. Once that is established, the chaos is no longer chaos, but something with structure and patterns. Now there is something with rules, and this can be understood and mastered.

Learning about how subtle energy works gives you the theoretical knowledge to interact on multiple levels, without losing balance. Energetic tools and techniques give you practical skills to maneuver the environment effectively and manipulate the subtle world the same way anyone would influence the material plane. Acceptance is central. Without it, little progress can be made. This means accepting yourself and the whole situation. Reversing the self-neglect and choosing to see yourself as worthy can take some time. Fear of being egotistical often gets in the way of self-love, but it's the ego that makes one question one's own worthiness. The difference between self-loathing and a healthy regard for oneself is night and day. It is the difference between feeling tortured and being at peace. Choose peace.

What being a sensitive means for an empath in years to come can often provoke anxiety and fear? This can be a miserable experience, where the mind dreams up a variety of potential worrisome situations that are rarely based in reality. Relax. It's a journey. Start at the beginning and let the rest unfold. Attend to what needs to be addressed now and learn to be ok with uncertainty. Life is unpredictable already, so why does having empathic traits make this any different? People often run from themselves, but where is there to run to? It's like a hamster on a wheel. A note of warning: People who ignore their gifts do not tend to fare well. Doing so is trying to escape a connection to something greater than yourself, and every individual always knows — on some level — that this is what they are choosing. It amounts to no more than burying one's head in the sand. Empaths who repress or ignore their experiences remain imbalanced and are never truly happy.

Our wise friend from Chapter 2, the mythological scholar Joseph Campbell, loves to talk about something he called "The Hero's Journey". Campbell claimed that myths from around the world relating a sort of hero's quest always have the same fundamental steps. It begins with the hero living a normal life and leaving home when he feels urged to do. This nudge from the universe is "The Call to Adventure". The hero then abandons the known world upon the answer of The Call, to undertake a mission in the uncharted territory of unknown and unexplored realms. On the journey, the hero faces tests, meets helpers, and — if successful — undergoes a personal transformation in which there is a newfound awareness and appreciation of the richness within.

The journey usually ends with the hero — now remarkably wiser from the ordeal — returning home, often to share their discoveries with humanity. This metaphor applies to any human who makes the bold decision to blaze their own path through the wilderness, in the attempt to find themselves and what life is really about. Most people never receive The Call (at least in this lifetime), and for those who do, there is a choice to make whether or not to embark on it in the first place. The thing is, there's no journey (and no prize) if the hero refuses to answer The Call to Adventure. This potential hero has chosen the safe path and will live the rest of their life with the sense that they missed out on their destiny.

Being an empath can be likened to receiving The Call. The choice of exploring a dimension to life that goes beyond the physical world is completely in your hands. If you choose to embrace your abilities, being proactive is incredibly important. So much of the suffering empaths endure is due to reacting to circumstances. The situation "hits them", throws them off balance, and the empath strains to make the discomfort go away. It's a vicious cycle. You may be so discouraged and exhausted that you struggle to find the strength to try to solve the problem. You may have become miserably content with managing symptoms, opposed to getting to the root of the problem. This is only putting on a band-aid and becoming proactive will put the empathy back in control. You will benefit greatly from looking at your life and identifying the dynamics of difficult as well as positive situations.

Taking special precautions and working with multiple techniques may be necessary to successfully navigate the fields of energy. When you know of a difficult situation or person is in the near future, it is important to take whatever steps you need to neutralize the situation, or even turn it into a positive exchange. Creating balance is the most complete way to thrive. This is embracing yourself as a whole being and operating on a physical, emotional, and spiritual level. People are multidimensional, and optimal functioning is experiencing wellness in all areas of life. Health is good, work is satisfying, relationships are positive, finances are stable, and a connection to divinity is strong. One feels content and purposeful. Balance is relative to the individual and situation, and what balances one will not always work for another.

Take some time to evaluate current circumstances and decide what is balanced and what requires attention. If you are interested in using something more scientific, plenty of avenues are waiting. Experimenting with an assortment of techniques is not a bad thing but trying to reinvent the wheel is usually a mistake. There are already a multitude of systems that teach how to balance the system. Whether it is Traditional Chinese Medicine, Ayurveda, philosophies behind martial arts, naturopathy, contemplative prayer, shamanism, crystal healing, reflexology, reiki, or mindfulness doesn't really matter. All of these modalities come with theory, guidelines, tools, and a progression of steps to balance the body.

The experimentation involves figuring out which paths bring results. Be careful about trying to utilize too many different schools of thought, however. Many techniques complement one another, but each path utilizes different theories that drives the philosophy as a whole. For example, tai chi teaches a completely different posture than yoga. Both methods work, and both techniques can be used, but it is impossible to follow one completely without contradicting the teachings of another. Another Zen parable describes trying to master two different disciplines as a hunter who chases two rabbits and catches neither. Many empaths naturally gravitate towards the helping professions or volunteering, and this can be a perfect way to use your heightened empathy and compassion in a constructive way. Once a sensitive finds a balancing point, the empathy loses its capacity for self-destruction. Instead, it is like sharing one's light with the world. Sensitive souls may be particularly suited to specific situations like working with the homeless, drug addicts, refugees, the terminally ill, or those displaced by natural disasters. Providing physical aid, comfort, and emotional support are wonderful ways to heal others and yourself. Animals may be more suited to certain empath's preferences, and environmental preservation could be perfect for another.

Empaths may provide spiritual guidance or direct their psychic sensitivities into such activities as astrology or intuitive readings. Engaging in important work is not always so obvious. The gift of sensitivity can be directed towards fellow human beings in any situation or calling. Working at a bank or gas station and treating every customer as a light-filled being is equally valuable. Consciously raising family and teaching kin the value of empathy can be most suitable. The key is finding a situation that matches your talents and interests. Feeling content is a sign that this has been achieved.

Loving-kindness meditations, also known as "Metta", come from the Buddhist tradition, and are designed to develop compassion. Cultivating a sense of love and reverence for all in the universe - with no desire to have this returned - is the goal. Loving-kindness is first directed at the self, because loving others is near impossible without self-love. The practices will help you further develop your gifts, as they continue to open your heart and prevent burnout.

HERE IS AN EXAMPLE OF HOW TO DO LOVING-KINDNESS MEDITATION

- Find a comfortable seat and take a few minutes to relax and become still.

- Focus on the heart center.

- Say, either mentally or out loud, "I am filled with loving-kindness". Picture yourself with a heart overflowing with love and generosity.

- Continue to repeat your affirmation and hold this imagery. Use any other words or visualizations that help support the sense of compassion. This should last fifteen to twenty minutes.

Practice regularly for a few weeks until you begin to feel its effects. Once a sense of loving-kindness for the self is established, move on to directing this energy towards others. The first five or ten minutes of the meditation remain directed at the self, but the rest will then be spent focusing on someone who summons forth feelings of love.

After practicing this for a few weeks, switch the focus from a loved one to someone neutral, possibly a stranger. This is a little more difficult. The most challenging step is sending loving-kindness towards someone who sparks feelings of hatred and animosity. With time, attitudes towards those who have brought harm into one's life will soften, and eventually be replaced with compassion and forgiveness.

REMEMBER

What happens to one happens to all. So, the greatest gift anyone can offer the world is their own wellness. The universe simultaneously carries individual and collective vibrations. A person's frequency is on a spectrum of positive and negative energy, and an individual's experience fluctuates as life circumstances change.

The strength of most people's light is medium, with some people casting weaker rays and other people casting stronger. This means that those with stronger vibrations are affecting the whole more significantly than those with feebler ones. The vibration can be anywhere on the spectrum of positivity and negativity, so someone with a strong vibration may be spreading good or bad energy.

There are a handful of souls in the world, most unknown, who shine forth such pure radiance that it counteracts most of the world's negativity and prevents mankind from plunging into darkness. Likewise, there exists incredibly malicious people who are harmful, and spread their hatred through mankind as a whole. With this concept in mind, flourishing as an empath is much weightier than one's own comfort. Whether or not you choose to publicly use your precious gifts is a personal decision, but — with proper balancing — honing your empathic traits and tendencies can only bring about good. Being compassionate in daily life is like infecting the world with joy. What may seem meager is not meager, not at all. Like a single lit candle, the smallest acts of kindness can vanquish the dark.

CHAPTER 10: HOW TO FIND THE RIGHT WORK THAT FEEDS YOU

Much of empath distress comes from work stress and hazards. They find difficult to fit in the competitive environment and become easily affected. Jobs including regular customer transactions brings extreme distress to empaths as they start focusing on people, they deal with rather than the work they are doing.

Considering this, choosing the right career path for the empath is very vital. Normally, empaths are expected to flourish in low-stress jobs or service-oriented works like teaching or medicine. Creativity attracts empaths, and they also prefer being self-employed. Empaths are often called "energy vampires" because of their unique ability of attracting energy from people around them.

PROFESSIONS BEST-SUITED FOR EMPATHS

Empaths perform great in professions that involve creativity and providing service. Works that can reflect the qualities of an empath in the real world are the ones best-suited for highly sensitive people. Helping professions, creative jobs, and self-employed business are preferred by the HSPs (highly sensitive person). They must make the most of their sensitivity to succeed in their workplace. It is easy for them to get swayed by the emotions of people around them including clients, patients, or colleagues, which is why low-stress jobs are more suitable for them.

- Healthcare professions like doctors, nurses, naturopaths, etc.
- Creative jobs like painting, writing, etc.
- Teaching
- Social and Public services
- Animal-related careers like animal sitters, pet specialists, etc.
- Working for non-profit organizations
- Counselling and mental health jobs like psychologists, counselors, therapists, rehabilitators, etc.

Empaths, as we already discussed before, are blessed with the dexterity of consuming energy from people around them - positive and negative. High-stress jobs like sales and marketing are perceived as too draining and emotionally destroying by empaths. Especially for empaths who are also introverts, customer dealings are extremely painful and mentally tiresome. Sensitive people who work in sales jobs often report to be feeling weary, and it is extremely difficult for them to deal with people the whole day. Researches on the mental health and well-being of empaths have clearly suggested the kind of jobs that are least suitable for them.

These jobs include:

- Sales, marketing and retail jobs like working in a store, or selling and gaining profits for the company
- Political jobs
- Public relation jobs like manager, recruiter, etc.

Being around people and dealing with them makes an empath overwhelmed. They lose focus on the job and invest all their energy in other people.

The best jobs for empaths are therefore the ones where they can get to invest more energy in themselves and work without being overwhelmed.

CHAPTER 11: THE WAYS OF DEVELOPING YOURSELF AS AN EMPATH

Living as an empath is difficult. No one understands your gift, and you feel constantly drained because everyone is pulling on your energy, and the truth is that sometimes you feel as if you are living in a nightmare!

The thing is, as I am sure you are well aware, you can't take the gift back to the shop to get a refund—it's yours for life. You can't turn your back on being an empath. It's not the same as a singing gift or an athletic gift where you can just decide that you are not going to sing or play basketball anymore. You have to learn to live a happy and productive life as an empath. So, here are some unique coping strategies to help you do this.

EMBRACE YOUR CREATIVE SIDE

Empaths are generally very creative people. They like to draw, paint, and dance, all of which can be very therapeutic. You have a desire to want to save the world from its many troubles, and while this is an admirable goal, the truth is that it's impossible. Expressing yourself through your creativity is a great way to eliminate negative energy and create something beautiful that you can control and be proud of.

It is also a way of purging some of the frustration that comes from not being able to heal the planet. Find something that you are good at and practice it daily. Incorporate your creativity into your daily routine and you will start to feel less stressed and frustrated about being an empath.

TURN YOUR HOME INTO A PROTECTIVE HAVEN

You should feel safe in your personal space; it is important that you create an environment that you are totally comfortable in. The mood and atmosphere of your home should reflect the way you feel inside. If you are not happy with your living quarters, you are going to have to make some changes.

What does your wardrobe look like? Your drawers? Underneath your bed? Are things just stuffed and piled up all over the place? As you have read, energy travels and attaches itself to objects, people, and other energy. When you are in an environment with a lot of negative people, you start feeling exhausted, hopeless, depleted, and distressed. When you are in an environment with positive people, you feel a sense of calm; you feel healthy and in control of your energy. Now let's take a look at how an untidy and tidy home can make you feel.

A CLUTTERED AND DIRTY HOME

Makes you feel exhausted. An untidy home is similar to an energy vampire. Negative energy attaches itself to objects, and simply being in such an environment will drain you.

Makes you feel hopeless. A never-ending pile of mess is psychologically overwhelming. You feel as if you will never get through it all so there is no point in even trying to clean it.

A TIDY AND ORGANIZED HOME

Makes you feel calm. You can relax and unwind in a tidy home. There is space to do things, and you know where everything is. When you walk into a hotel room, you immediately feel a sense of peace because the environment is tidy and organized.

Makes you feel healthy. Dust and mold accumulate in messes.

Are you always coughing and sneezing? Do you suffer from allergies? It's probably because you are breathing in all the dirt in your home. Give your home a spring clean and your health issues will improve.

Makes you feel in control. How does it feel when you know where everything is?

Clutter prevents positive energy from flowing through your home. Remember, energy attaches itself to objects, and negative energy is attracted to mess, which creates exhaustion, stagnation, and exasperation.

What does it feel like when negative energy is stuck in your body? You want to lie in bed and shut the world away because everything becomes more difficult and you can't explain why.

You will become more vibrant. Once you create harmony and order in your home, you will feel more radiant and present. Like acupuncture, which removes imbalances and blockages from the body to create more wellness and dynamism, clearing clutter removes imbalances and blockages from your personal space. When you venture through spaces that have been set ablaze with fresh energy, you are captured by inspiration, and the most attractive parts of your personality come to life.

You will get rid of bad habits and introduce good ones. All bad habits have triggers. Do you lie on your bed to watch TV instead of sitting on the couch because you can't be bothered to fold the laundry that has piled up over the past six months? Or because the bed represents sleep, and when you come home from work and get into bed, you are going to fall asleep instead of doing those important tasks on your to-do list. Once you tidy the couch, coming home from work will allow you to sit on it to watch your favorite TV program but get up once it's finished and do what you need to do.

You will improve your problem-solving skills. When your home has been opened up with a clear space, it's easier to focus, which provides you with a fresh perspective on your problems.

You will sleep better. Are you always tired no matter how much sleep you get? That's because negative energy is stuck under your bed amongst all that junk you've stuffed under there. Once you tidy up your bedroom, you will find that positive energy can flow freely around your room making it easier for you to have a deep and restful sleep.

You will have more time. Mess delays you. An untidy house means you are always losing things. You can't find a shoe, a sock, or your keys, so you waste time searching for them, which makes you late for work or social gatherings. When you declutter your home, you could save about an hour a day because you will no longer need to dig through a stack of items to find things.

Your intuition will be stronger. A clear space creates a sense of certainty and clarity. You know where everything is, so you have peace of mind. When you have peace of mind, you can focus on being in the present moment. When you need to make important decisions, you will find it easier to do so. It might take some time to give your home a deep clean, but you won't be sorry for it once it's done.

DAILY YOGA

Yoga is a powerful method to help get rid of unwanted energy. The combination of postures, deep breathing, and relaxation are essential to releasing tension and blocked energy. To release yourself from holding onto pain, whether it's yours or someone else's, you must let your life force travel freely within your body. So, here are a few tips to get you started. You can also buy books, DVDs, or join a yoga class.

BASIC BREATHING TECHNIQUE

- Sit on the ground, cross your legs, straighten your back, and place your hands over your knees.
- Close your eyes and take a deep breath in through your nose your stomach should rise when you do this.
- Hold your breath for four seconds.
- Breathe out for four seconds your stomach should deflate when you do this.
- Repeat this for five minutes.

YOGA POSES TO RELEASE NEGATIVE EMOTIONS

Here are three yoga poses to help you release negative energy and allow positive energy to flow freely throughout your body.

Facing Upwards Dog

To get rid of unwanted emotions, effective communication is essential. This yoga position helps to relieve tension in the throat and unblock and balance the throat chakra.

- Lay a mat down on the floor.

- Lie on your stomach, extend your legs behind you, and push the front of your feet into the ground.
- Position your hands flat on the mat directly underneath your shoulders.
- Inhale and use your hands to push your upper body up off the ground.
- Once you are in an upwards position, exhale.
- Stay like this for 10 seconds at the same time inhaling and exhaling.

Angle Bound Pose

Much of our emotional energy and trauma is held in our hips. The angle bound pose will loosen up your hips and help move stuck energy throughout the body.

- Sit in a crossed leg position on your mat but allow the soles of your feet to touch.
- Place your hands over your feet and split them apart as if you are opening a book.
- Take a deep breath in and stretch your spine upwards.
- Exhale and relax your knees allowing them to fall towards the ground.
- Repeat this for 10 breaths.

The Plank Pose

The plank pose helps to strengthen your core, and it is good for the central nervous system. When our bodies feel strong, we also feel strong emotionally and mentally, which allows you to cope with any challenges that may come your way.

- Lie on your stomach with your palms on the floor directly under your shoulders.
- Your legs should be extended behind you (shoulder width apart) with the balls of your toes pressing into the ground.
- Inhale and push your entire body off the ground using your hands and feet.
- Remain in this position for 10 seconds at the same time inhaling and exhaling.

One of the things that empaths dislike about their gift is that it makes them feel cluttered. They pick up emotions and energy from everywhere, and they want to escape from it all. You are constantly bombarded with stress and negativity, whether it's from people or through the media, and your one desire is to get away.

Empaths find it difficult to separate their true identity from the emotions of others. You are very idealistic and are constantly thinking of ways to improve the lives of others. This strong desire to help people can become compulsive. If you are not an empath and are reading this, you now understand why your friend is so obsessive when it comes to finding solutions to your problems. When listening to a problem, empaths will often come up with an immediate solution and do everything in their power to help fix it. Although this is a good quality to have, it can lead empaths to become emotionally co-dependent because you are constantly relying on the happiness of others to feel satisfied.

The assumption is that there is only one type of co-dependency, which is where a person is emotionally or financially reliant upon an individual to take care of them. Another form of co-dependency is when a person's satisfaction in life is derived from their ability to please and help other people. This is the type of co-dependency that empaths often suffer from. If you read any books about co-dependency, you will find the characteristics of an unskilled empath described on every page, including:

- Feeling guilt, pity, and anxiety when other people are experiencing problems
- The belief that you are responsible for the choices, well-being, needs, wants, actions, and feelings of others
- Wondering why they don't receive the same treatment from others
- Not knowing how or when to verbalize their wants and needs because they don't know what they are and they don't view them as important as everyone else's
- Doing things for other people that they don't want to do and then getting angry about it

- Feeling compelled to help people whether they ask for it or not and refusing to accept help from others because they feel guilty
- Feeling sad because they pour so much into others, but they don't receive the same back from others
- Feeling empty or useless when they don't have a problem or crisis to resolve or someone to help
- Needy people are always attracted to them
- Putting others' needs before their own
- Feeling used, unappreciated, victimized, and angry

These co-dependent characteristics describe the unskilled empath because empaths have an innate inclination to want to make things better; they are natural healers. But putting so much energy into restoring and pleasing other people is emotionally draining. Empaths need to cut themselves off from this behavior and understand that happiness comes from within and nowhere else.

For example, Mike comes home from work after a bad day, and instead of greeting his wife, he stomps up the stairs, goes into his room, and slams the door. Susan, his wife, is an empath, and she automatically detects that there is something wrong because she starts to feel his pain. She does everything she can think of to make him feel better, but nothing works. Every day, he comes home in the same bad mood. Susan spends her days looking for solutions to a problem she doesn't understand, and her evenings trying to implement them. Her life is centered around her husband and improving his mood. This is what co-dependence is like for an empath. Susan can break her back trying to rectify her husband's problem, but if he is unwilling to talk about it and it is due to a stressful situation at work, until he decides to open up or do something about it himself, there is nothing she can do to help him. The real solution is that Susan must learn to live independently from her husband's problems.

Have you been through a similar experience? Maybe the emotions of others are making it difficult for you to get things done. When you run into situations like this, you need to evaluate the problem to see where it is coming from because, like the example with Mike and Susan, there are going to be times when there is nothing you can do to actively resolve the situation. Your only option will be to offer your support and give your friend or partner the space to deal with their issues. Since you are an energy sponge, you should keep your distance from that person until they have gotten over the crisis. You can still support them without compromising your emotional wellbeing.

CHAPTER 12: GUIDED MEDITATION FOR CLEANSING AND CLEARING YOUR ENERGY

This thirty-minute session is meant to reboot your entire system. Feel the energy flow through you to completely rejuvenate your mind, body, and spirit. You will leave feeling ready to go and face the world. Enjoy!

Welcome to your *Cleansing and Clearing Energy* guided meditation...

Find a comfortable position in a quiet place, seated or lying

calm your breath...

Close your eyes... and gently fill your lungs with fresh air...

Feel it inside...

Take a deep breath again...

Slowly inhaling and exhaling...

Close your eyes and imagine that you are in a field of black eyed Susans...

Together they make a field of yellow, with little black specks canvassing the surface...

The field is bright and sunny,

feel the warmth of the sun's rays on your face as it emerges from behind a puffy, white cloud.

Feel the smile grow on your cheeks as the breeze whisks away your stress and emotions...

Hear the breeze rustling through the flowers, touching on every petal...

Hear the sounds of crickets chirping in between the leaves...

They are so busy, and you are so still...

See the swallows flitting their wings just above the flowers...

They sing and accept the energy from the sun as well...

Everything is in perfect harmony at this moment...

A small, half-grown black eyed Susans catches your eye, just in front of you...

It is much smaller than those around it, yet perfect just the same...

You look at its face as the breeze gently tests its long stem...

Each petal is perfectly symmetrical around its center, except for one...

This is its imperfection, letting the universe know who it is, why it is special...

Each petal is a bright golden yellow, with perfect, crisp edges... and a bone down the middle...

They stretch far out from the center as if reaching out toward its other flower companions...

The dew from the morning still sits in the crevices of the flower, around its black center...

Each droplet catches and reflects the light, bringing a jewel-like quality over the flower...

You begin to hear a soft buzzing sound, slowly emerging from the distance...

It circles around you. It is a honeybee, looking for the perfect flower...

It hovers around a few flowers before landing gently and gracefully on the flower in front of you...

The stem bends just slightly with the added weight...

You turn your focus to this minuscule honeybee with its plump body and golden yellow hair...

It looks soft to the touch underneath its luminescent wings...

The bee is calm for a moment, before attending to its work...

It stops and drinks from the tiny water droplets coating the petals...

You meet your breath with that of the bee, connecting on a spiritual level...

You are both equally enjoying this flower, and that is all there is, frozen in time...

For a moment this connection is powerful and strong...

Just as quickly as it came, the bee pushes off the flower and disappears into the meadow...

You focus your attention out back onto the field...

You appreciate the stark contrast between the bright golden flowers and the blue sky as your backdrop...

You continue to look around, unable to fully soak in the beauty of this scenery...

Your eyes close, and all your senses focus on the sound of the crickets...

Each chirp like a melody floating on in the background of your brain...

All you feel is the warmth of the sun cascading over your shoulders...

Everything is calm and focused in this moment...

As you sit in that field, you feel your bottom connected with the earth...

Feel the energy flowing up through the bottom of your spine...

As you breathe in, accept this energy wholeheartedly from the earth...

As you exhale, feel all of your negative energy flow out, as the earth accepts it...

With each breath, you are renewed with a revitalizing energy...

It can hardly be contained...

You are refreshed, renewed, and you feel this new energy coursing through every inch of you...

Through your spine, down to each and every fingertip...

You are vibrating, your spirit ready to drive your physical body, ready to propel it forward…

Open your eyes…

Recognize where you are in your quiet space…

Feel the energy coursing through your body, just as in the imagery. This energy is real. You have connected spiritually with this universal energy, and it is ready to propel you forward…

Take a few deep breaths, readying your body for movement…

Now get up and carry out your day using the energy the universe has given you. Do good with that energy…

CHAPTER 13: GUIDED MEDITATION FOR SHIELDING AND BOUNDARY SETTING MEDITATION FOR EMPATHS

Welcome to this guided meditation for empaths, to help setting shielding and boundaries

First, we're going to relax with a few deep breaths...

Slowly breathe in allowing your belly to expand followed by your chest so that your lungs are completely full of air...

Take about 5 seconds to do this...

This now pass and hold the breath for 5 seconds finally...

slowly breathe out over the course of 5 seconds...

using your diaphragm to put out any remaining air

The length of time for each stage of breathing is not important as long as it is done in equal measure...

Repeat this process several times to deep in your relaxation

if you haven't already, please close your eyes...

Very good...

You may now allow your breath to return to its natural rhythm...

visualize a circle around you...

Think of this circle as going around your whole body, protecting you from emotions and ideas that aren't your own.

This circle is full of light

It will serve as an imaginary boundary...

Despite this being a mental activity, your mind is powerful enough to commit to this boundary you're setting.

Add more detail to it...so that it can work better...

Picture this circle of light around you...

As a set of rules that you apply to yourself...

Bring mentally all the thoughts and emotions within that circle...

determine all the thoughts and emotions that belong to you...

consider your own worries and anxieties and mark them as your own...

These things within the circle are all coming from you without the influence of others.

On that same note, everything outside the circle doesn't belong to you,

These are the things that you pick up from other people...

Noticing someone hit the table in anger

Hearing a hint of aggression from someone over the phone

Getting a glimpse of a frown

Sensing some authority from a speaker

All these things do not go through that circle, and if it's not within the circle, they shouldn't go through...

You can block off any negativity coming your way because you aren't focused on dealing with the emotions of others but on dealing with whatever is in your circle...

When these boundaries become clear and more established, this circle of light isn't just a circle anymore...

It becomes a wall that protects you from influences that you do not welcome into your person...

Take a moment to sit and observe how you are filling...

Slowly that your awareness expands to your immediate surroundings as you return fully to your body...

When you're ready open your eyes...

How do you feel now, compared to before the meditation?

Did anything shift?

Set for as long as you like to observe what's going on for you...

Thank you and namaste.

Considered a useful tool even for non-empaths, mindfulness harnesses your mind's capacity to shift focus. For an empath, this could be difficult with all the influences you can absorb. But with proper training, you can develop this skill and use it as instant relief from the many emotions you encounter every day.

Like mental imagery, mindfulness meditation forces you to stop thinking about feelings that aren't yours as you shift focus to the sensations that you're personally feeling right that moment.

It begins the same way, by finding a nice quiet corner wherein you can focus. This time, instead of bringing an image to mind, you appreciate your surroundings and live in the moment.

You begin by closing your eyes and focusing on one area at a time. Start with your feet. As you're seated with your eyes closed, focus your attention to your feet. Don't just feel the floor through your shoes. Feel your toes inside your socks. You can choose to wiggle your toes if it helps you focus on them.

As you focus on your feet, recognize the sensations you're feeling. Are your socks warm enough around your feet? How does the fabric feel on your foot? Be sure to account for both feet as you feel them on the ground.

Once you're done with the feet, move upward to your legs. How does the fabric of your pants or shorts feel against your legs? Is it letting your skin breath or is it constricting? Are your bare legs exposed? Is there a breeze coming through your legs? Don't comment on the status of your legs but focus on what your legs are feeling right that moment.

Do the same thing with your hands and arms as you move upward. If your hands and arms are resting on something, try to put those sensations into words as you meditate. As you move through various parts of your body, you'll notice that you're slowly living in the moment while realizing the many sensations that you usually take for granted. That is the premise of mindfulness. You forget about what you're thinking and just focus on what is going right that moment. This may be hard to do if you're a beginner, but it gets easier with repetition and constant practice.

One thing that could disrupt your meditation is your own mind. It is inevitable to sometimes drift into your own thoughts in the middle of meditation and start to think inward. But you shouldn't let this disrupt your rhythm. Slowly remind yourself of what you're doing and start over. There's nothing wrong with getting lost in your thoughts, you just need to know how to guide yourself back and refocus.

Interestingly, you don't always have to focus on the moment and the sensations you're feeling. Mindfulness meditation can also be done with your breath.

Instead of thinking about your various body parts, you can visualize your lungs and your diaphragm as you take in breaths. Visualize the air coming into your lungs as it is absorbed into your bloodstream. Take as many breaths as you want to create the full image in your head.

The whole process should not take more than five minutes to fully refresh your senses. At the end of the meditation, you're back in the moment without any thought about other people's emotions and stress.

CHAPTER 14: GUIDED MEDITATION EMPATH ENERGY & EMOTION REALIGNMENT & PROTECTION

30 MINUTE BODY ENERGY

Welcome to your *Body Energy* guided meditation...

Get into a comfortable position...

This could seat with your legs crossed or lie down in Savasana yoga pose...

Close your eyes... and gently fill your lungs with fresh air...

Feel it inside...

Take a deep breath again...

Take your focus to your body...

Notice your breath, and simply notice the way that you breathe...

In your mind's eye notice how your breath flows in and then flows out of your body...

If you notice your attention beginning to wander around...

Gently bring it back to focus on your breathing...

When you inhale you are bringing life force, vitality, and energy into your body...

When you exhale you are releasing fatigue, negativity, and stress from your body...

Allow these negative energies to drain out through your feet and disappear...

Breathe in and breathe out...

Continue to stay with deep, cleansing inhales and exhales, and take ten more...

With each of your inhales you are bringing in more energy to your body...

Feel this new subtle energy vibration spreading throughout your body...

all the way from your feet up to your head...

and from your head down to your feet...

Become aware of this tingling and warmth in every cell...

Begin to visualize the positive energy that has begun to accumulate throughout your body and these energies shining as bright as the sun...

Take this shining, glowing energy all the way to your crown at the top of your head...

Take a deep breath in and release slowly...

At the top of your head start to feel the warmth of this positive energy as it starts to radiate over your neck and face...

Feel this new peacefulness and lightness in mind...

Take another deep breath in and slowly let it out...

Notice the positive energy moving across your neck and shoulders, down both arms all the way to the fingertips, and across to your heart center...

Feel this love and warmth feeling your heart...

Let this positive healing energy to fill your body with unconditional love...

Take a deep cleansing breath...

Now notice the healing energy moving down your body over your hips and down both legs to the tips of your toes...

Fell how this energy helps to ground you to the earth...

Feel supported, centered, and grounded...

Take another cleansing breath...

Your entire body is filled with this positive energy...

Allow this energy to flow through your entire body freely...

With every breath you take to let this energy grow stronger...

Take three more deep, cleansing breaths…

Focus your attention on your breathing and feel how this positive energy flows through your body…

Pay attention of this new sense of alertness and clarity in your mind, vitality and energy in your body, and peacefulness and positivity in your soul…

Let this positivity awaken your soul…

Take a cleansing breath…

Rest here with your breath and these feelings for the rest of your meditation…

Now let the awareness take over…

Start to listen to the sounds around you…

Bring your attention back to all your body…

Pay attention to your toes and start moving them…

Pay attention to your neck and start moving it…

Pay attention to the fingers of your hands and start moving them…

Open gently your eyes…

Inhale deeply and slowly drift back to full consciousness…

Welcome back and Namaste…

Welcome to your *Emotional Realignment* guided meditation...

Find a comfortable position, seated or lying...

Close your eyes... and gently fill your lungs with fresh air...

Feel it inside...

Take a deep breath again...

Start to become aware of your breath...

Notice the sensation of the breath as it enters through your nose with a cool sensation... and then as it warms as it travels gently into your lungs...

Fill up your lungs with a deep inhale, bringing in prana, energy, and vitality, your life force...

While you exhale, feel how your body is releasing negativity, stress, and toxins that may have accumulated during your day...

Stay with your breath and focus on this feeling of deep inner peace for ten more inhales and exhales...

Feel this positive energy that you have coursing through your body...

Notice how every cell is tingling and warming...

Notice the energy that is in your surrounding environment, in all parts of nature... and in all living things...

Take all of these energies and bring them together so that they feel as one...

Picture these energies shining as bright as the sun...

Allow this ball of white shining energy into your crown at the top of your head...

Then allow this white light to travel down your body...

Notice how it is slowly warming your face and neck... and the traveling over your shoulders and down your arms and fingers...

Notice as it moves across your chest, down your stomach... and over your hips, and then spreads down your legs, feet, and toes...

Your body is now filled with this warm, divine, white energy and light...

Allow this healing light to fill every part of your body that needs to be healed...

Feel all of its healing and warmth spreading throughout your surrounds...

Let this light bring you healing... and peace to any emotional traumas or issues you may have...

Shift your awareness to any desires or intentions that you may currently have...

Hold onto these thoughts of your desires... and intentions as you let this energy bring you your deepest wishes to life and your intentions to reality...

Feel how you are now connected to this divine light and energy... and remember that all is one...

Stay with this new feeling of peacefulness, relaxation, and deepness for the remainder of your meditation...

Don't move, just let the awareness take over...

Start to listen to the sounds around you...

Bring your attention back to all your body...

Pay attention to your toes and start moving them...

Pay attention to your neck and start moving it...

Pay attention to the fingers of your hands and start moving them...

Open gently your eyes...

Inhale deeply and slowly drift back to full consciousness...

Welcome back and Namaste...

CONSULT YOUR DOCTOR BEFORE TRYING AN ADVANCED MEDITATION TECHNIQUE

The meditation techniques contained in this book are basic. But, if you decide to practice advanced techniques such as kundalini meditation later on, it's best to consult your doctor especially if you're suffering from a mental health problem such as depression. Do not meditate right after eating as this may affect your ability to focus. And most importantly, be kind to yourself. It's impossible to master meditation in just a few hours, days, and weeks. Be patient.

Meditation is a powerful relaxation technique. But, if you're an empath, you'll need tools to help you reap the maximum benefits of meditation.

CRYSTALS

Crystals are beautiful and colorful. They have strong healing properties. They have the ability to remove stress and tension from your body. They can subtly change your health, energy, and aura.Crystals can do a lot of things – they can increase your ability to forgive yourself and others. These crystals can remove the emotional blockages caused by fear and self-doubt. These crystals balance your energy, so they're considered as first-rate meditation tools. These crystals calm your mind and help you reap the full benefits of meditation.

ROSE QUARTZ

Rose quartz is known as the crystal of love. This beautiful pink precious stone carries a soft, feminine energy that exudes love, compassion, and peace. If you're an empath, finding true love can be a challenge so this stone could greatly benefit you.The rose quartz also inspires you to practice self-love and put yourself above anyone else's need. This stone heals your heart chakra and it has a strong purifying effect that flushes out all the heartaches and negative energies. It also balances the yin-yang energy in your body and improves your overall mental well-being.

MALACHITE

This has a healing energy that removes emotional blockages. It protects your core being, especially during challenging times.

AMETHYST

Many empaths have strong intuition and yet, they do not trust this intuition most of the time. This beautiful purple stone heightens an empath's intuition and encourages them to trust their gut feelings.

BLACK TOURMALINE

This has a powerful protective energy that pushes all the negative energy away. This stone is an important stone that empathic healers must have.

BLUE TOPAZ

Many empaths feel that their needs are not as important as the needs of the people around them. This stone helps you think clearly, and it empowers you communicate your personal truth. It helps you see the big picture and remove the tension and stress caused by relationships, work, or social interactions.

LAPIS LAZULI

This beautiful blue stone has an intense color and appearance. It also has an intense protective power that can guard you from negative energies. This stone will help you not to take things personally and it helps clear your mind.

UNAKITE

Your emotions can be overwhelming sometimes, and this can take a toll on your physical and emotional health. Unakite is a rare stone that can help balance your emotions. It also helps you connect with the Energy Source and improve your spirituality.

PURPLE JADE

This is a great protective stone for empaths because it aligns and balances your energy, keeping the negative energies in check.

ESSENTIAL OILS

The aroma of essential oils can help reset your body and strengthen your spirit. It can also help create a peaceful atmosphere during meditation. Here's a list of essential oils that you can use when you're meditating:

LAVENDER

Lavender has a mesmerizing sweet scent that you can't get enough of. It helps improve your mood and improves your sleep. This oil is also useful for empaths who suffer from neurological issues such as stress, depression, and anxiety. You can spray this oil around your room before your meditation practice. You can use it as a perfume, too.

CEDARWOOD

Cedarwood has a fresh scent. It has a cooling and calming effect on the body. This oil reduces the symptoms of stress, depression, and anxiety. Its scent also induces the release of a happy hormone called serotonin, making you feel giddy, relaxed, and happy.

SANDALWOOD

If you feel anxious all the time, it would be beneficial to use sandalwood essential oil during your meditation practice. This oil also helps prevent mental sluggishness and increase your alertness. This oil improves your cognitive function, too, and protects you from dementia. It decreases the symptoms of depression, too.

PATCHOULI

This oil helps ward off negative feelings such as anger, anxiety, and sadness. It is also a powerful sedative. It helps you relax and sleep after a long tiring day.

BASIL

Basil increases your mental alertness and decreases the symptoms of anxiety. It decreases mental fatigue, depression, and migraines. It helps you achieve clarity and increase your mental strength.

CHAMOMILE

This raises your spirits and helps you fight depression. It also reduces mental sluggishness and nervousness.

BERGAMOT

This oil is a powerful relaxant. It helps relieve stress, tension, and anxiety. It also helps cure depression.

YLANG YLANG

If you're looking for a feel-good oil, this is it. This essential oil is a natural remedy for depression. It expands your heart and it helps you release negative emotions such as anger and jealousy. It also increases your self-esteem. It also increases your self-awareness and promotes self-love.

ROSE

This essential oil is a potent aphrodisiac and it helps improve one's self-confidence, self-esteem, and mental strength.

GINGER

Ginger oil increases your energy. It is a powerful remedy for the emotional and mental issues that empaths go through such as depression, stress, restlessness, anxiety, and mental exhaustion.

LEMON

Lemon essential oil increases your energy and it helps curb your appetite, so it keeps you from turning to food when you're stressed.

ROSEMARY

This one can do wonders to your mental health. It reduces oxidative stress and it increases your mental clarity. It helps you become more decisive and less overwhelmed by life's small challenges.

FRANKINCENSE

Frankincense relieves stress and help fight anxiety. It increases your spiritual connection and it also strengthens your intuition. When you feel overwhelmed, this oil reduces and stabilizes your heart rate.

TEA TREE

Tea Tree oil has anti-cancer benefits. It is powerful because it removes the malignancy of the plasma tracts or chakras. It helps restore the natural vibrational frequency of your chakras.

GERANIUM

This oil reduces the symptoms of depression and stress. It calms your nerves and relaxes your mind.

EUCALYPTUS

Empaths are prone to mental exhaustion. Eucalyptus can help them deal with that because this oil has a refreshing and cooling effect. It is also a stimulant which helps remove mental sluggishness and exhaustion. So, if you are tired after a day of dealing with different people at work, use eucalyptus oil during our meditation practice.

NEROLI

Neroli is a great aphrodisiac. But it does more than awaken your sexuality and bring back the wild moments of your youth. This oil releases anxiety and depression. It is a powerful tool that can help you relax during meditation.

CINNAMON

Empaths usually feel tired all the time because of all that negative energy that they get from people around them. This is the reason why cinnamon oil is beneficial for empaths. This essential oil increases your energy and it also strengthens your immune system and it helps treat depression, too.

CITRONELLA

Citronella oil is primarily known as a repellant. But, it also has a powerful anti-anxiety because it relieves negative feelings. This oil induces strong feelings of hope and happiness.

GERANIUM

Geranium is a beautiful summer flower. This oil is a commonly used in aromatherapy. It is used for holistic treatment. Geranium reduces depression and relieves stress. It also decreases nervous tension and promotes strong feelings of well-being and peace.

Meditation is a powerful tool that you can use to achieve peace of mind. It is a tool that you can use to silence the noise around you. It allows you to make better decisions. It also enables you to build an energetic shield that protects you from all the negativity around you. It is a powerful technique that you can use to take back control in your life and protect yourself from all the unpleasant things in the world.

The journey to realizing your full potential as an empath can be riddled with challenges and hardships. You may be confused at first, but you will greatly appreciate your gift once you learn more about it. Even Albert Einstein was a great believe in the power of intuition. The imagination and creativity in listening to one's intuition leads to new discoveries.

Once you have mastered your capabilities as an empath, you can become a channel of good energies to those around you. You will be able to effectively protect yourself and other people with your empathic abilities. Your life can be filled with the joy of appreciating the world and having a raised level of awareness.

If you experienced trauma and addiction as an empath, you can turn your life around and become a healthy empath. When you heal others, you are also healing yourself.

You can harness this inner power and transform it to help you become successful in fulfilling your destiny. It can help you to lead other people, whether this means spiritual leadership or a leader in the workplace.

You must have a strong commitment to nurture your empathic abilities. You must allow yourself to learn---accept that there is so much to know about this blessing from nature. Only if you open your mind to the exponential possibilities of your empathic power can you make it grow and not cause it to be an issue in your life.

All the best!

Part III

OPEN YOUR THIRD EYE

A Real Guide to: Open Your Third Eye; Activate Your Pineal Gland; Expand the power of Your Mind; Attain Higher Consciousness; Find Spiritual Enlightenment; Develop Psychic Abilities; Engage Astral Travel; and Derive Intuition through Meditation.

It's one thing to strip yourself down to an elemental level, it's another thing to build yourself back up. You are more than what you see; within you there are a trillion connections, bulging with the complexity of a billion galaxies. You may have read articles and books describing the incredible abilities of the brain, or how the human eyesight is sharper than the lens of the most advanced cameras, or how your thighs have a tensile strength greater than that of concrete. The vast peculiarities of the human make-up are truly mind-blogging.

However, all the wonders are merely physical. There is an entire realm of awareness that transcends the physical confines of your body. It's a realm brimming with knowledge, enlightenment, and indescribable wonders, but to access this realm and find the truest form of balance within yourself, you must attain Higher Consciousness. It is in the quest for this that the significance of learning to access and open your third eye begins to shine through.

The third eye has an intricate, rich history. From the iconography of the Hindu deity Shiva, who had a vertical third eye and hair aflame with snakes (snakes were regarded as a pointer to chakra in focused body points and were revered in Hindu and Buddhist spiritual practice) to the eye of Ra and the eye of Horus in Egyptian religious mythos, the third eye was a powerful symbol of enlightenment, out-of-body experience, spiritual authority, and even clairvoyance. As a precursor to spiritual vision, ancestors of the Hindu religious culture—immersed in their quest for a spiritual awakening—would tattoo a third eye right in the middle of their foreheads, where the third eye was believed to be situated.

The third eye is the gate to spiritual enlightenment, and, in this book, you shall gain not only an intellectual understanding of this highly important spiritual appendage but also receive guidelines on how to gain a direct experience with it. Because of the raw and unbounded power of spiritual vision, it would normally be out of reach to us as mortals. However, through dedicated work, practice, and consistent discipline, we can find the keys to the gate and open up portals to a higher world. Many people feel boxed in by their bodies. It's like a vessel that simply won't budge; one that confines you into the most basic plane of human existence. Which is why, over the centuries, we have walked the path of enlightenment, seeking answers to burning questions, wetting our palate of curiosity with the sweetness of knowledge, and finding new ways to establish a connection with the core of our being on a higher plane.

With the third eye, you do not have to be bound to the limitations of the physical; you do not have to endure the restrictions of an earthly tether that is frail, slow, and lacking in the speed and strength with which you can credit lower animals. The third eye grants you the ability to reach, interact with, and even take charge of higher levels of consciousness. The third eye is like a living being in itself, in that it guides you through the process of making decisions in your daily life, exposing you to an unconventional perception of the world around you and leading the way, especially when human intuition fails.

With concentration and meditation, you can soar beyond the physical, and the third eye is the vehicle that will get you there. First, though, you must let go of limiting beliefs. There's a famous narrative that Hollywood has championed over the years, one that suggests that as human beings we only use ten percent of our brainpower. Neurologists may argue the factual accuracy of this idea till the end of time, but one thing that stands out is that it only further establishes the understanding that even at our very physical best we still are barely scratching the surface of our truest potential. The third eye is your go to for inner peace, for foresight, for a feeling of constant evolution happening from the inside, for change, for enhanced cognition, and for so much more.

So, the question becomes:

- What is this third eye?
- And how do I find it?

The response takes us back many centuries, to the time of a Greek doctor and philosopher called Galen. At that time, other doctors and thinkers like Galen began to develop an affinity for the pineal gland. They regarded it as the seat of the soul and attributed supernatural characteristics to it. They believed that the pineal gland was in charge of the flow of an ethereal substance which they termed 'psychic pneuma' or 'the first instrument of the soul'. Galen didn't subscribe to this claim. If anything, he believed they were completely flawed, that the pineal gland was merely a tiny organ that regulated blood flow. Unbeknownst to him however, by publishing a document to discredit their opinions, what he effectively did was set the pace for a widespread resurgence of spiritual awareness among people. Then came René Descartes, who not only reinforced the critical relevance of the pineal gland, but further tagged it the 'principal seat of the soul'. He believed that all thoughts originated from the pineal gland, and that it was the confluence point where stimuli and information absorbed by the two physical eyes were synthesized and transmitted to the soul. He was of the belief that the mind could be separated from the body, and that it was all due to the pineal gland, especially because it is unique by virtue of not being in a pair like most sensory organs.

The pineal gland has proven to be a very integral part of the human body over the years, as many schools of thought agree that it holds a certain relevance that cannot be explained through the physical. In fact, certain theosophists have posited that the third eye and pineal gland are one and the same, arguing that the pineal gland simultaneously serves physical and spiritual functions.

Shiva and other deities of the religion of Hinduism further spread third eye awareness, especially in the imagery associated with Kundalini Yoga. Shiva was a highly complex deity, as he was both destroyer and restorer at the same time. His right eye was thought to be the sun and the left, the moon, but his third eye stood out, not only as a physical uniqueness, but also as his key to knowledge and wisdom. With his third eye, he could see far ahead and beyond the apparent, vanish all surrounding evil forces, and protect good people from evildoers.

The Hindus of India believed strongly that the third eye was the gate to inner worlds. In their fire rituals, for instance, the coconut carried deep symbolic significance. Every coconut has three evenly spaced depressions naturally engraved at the top of its outer shell. They considered these to be the three eyes, two of which were believed to be blind because they couldn't be opened to reach the milk on the inside, so that all the energy of vision flowed to the third eye, which could be punctured to reach the fruit on the inside, causing it to radiate with power. In this light, the third eye was seen as the one and only pathway to access one's most authentic self, by expanding the realm of one's consciousness and causing one to gain a new, powerful perspective.

THE AJNA CHAKRA

Ajna is a Sanskrit word for the sixth chakra, which is also known as the third eye chakra. It is anatomically located in the brain, above the base of the nose. This chakra is credited with enabling its user to achieve clear thought, undiluted self-reflection, and spiritual contemplation. This chakra is powerful in that through it you may view the outer world and inner world at the same time; internalizing the outer while externalizing the inner.

Through our connection to the divine, we all hold deep truths on our insides. With the energy of the third eye, we are able to pierce through illusions and transcend the limiting duality of right and wrong. The Ajna chakra is also credited with integrated thinking, as it helps balance the functionalities of both hemispheres of the brain, hybridizing the analytical and logical thinking of the left hemisphere with the synergized and creative thinking of the right hemisphere, seamlessly.

The Ajna chakra is linked with the color indigo, which is why if you have come across any users of the power of the third eye you may have observed that they favor the colors purple and indigo. The Ajna chakra has been known to guide the spheres of life that govern metaphorical sight, intuition, perception of physical and spiritual realities, and mental guidance. Even further, the Ajna chakra is capable of healing the senses, purifying thought, taste, hearing, and of course vision.

Most folk live all their lives with this superbly powerful energy force lying dormant in them, never finding use. Such people live through their entire lifespans on the most basic plane of existence. For some others, however, harmful practices and beliefs have activated their third eye chakras but, rather than being in sync, caused the energy to reverse in an unnatural direction or further created mental blockages that limit the flow of their spiritual energies. When the third eye chakra is blocked or reversed, one tends to experience highly negative sensations, such as a perpetual feeling of stagnancy, insomnia, migraines, depression, mental disorders, jarring flashbacks, paranoia, irritation, addiction, perpetual cynicism, and an undying feeling of 'no connection' with the world and all that it contains.

THE FOREHEAD DOT

Certain leaps in research and fresh discoveries by Egyptologists in the last two decades have brought to light the understanding that human awareness of the third eye has existed much longer than the average person might think. In Egypt, the word 'Aten' was used to describe the red forehead dot that worshippers of the sun deity, Ra, sometimes donned. It was a symbol of the sun, but its underlying spiritual ideologies suggest a core similarity with the Ajna chakra in Kundalini Yoga and the third eye in Hinduism.

The people of ancient Egypt understood duality. They understood that, for peace to be assured, opposing forces had to be balanced. Some believe that they gained this insight from the river Nile, which separated Egypt into two lands; Upper and Lower Egypt. Both lands were basically polar opposites. Upper Egypt was elevated while Lower Egypt was generally marshy land. There were vast differences in their techniques of pottery, flint making, weapon manufacturing, and sculpture. The people of Lower Egypt also derived much of their sustenance through fishing and hunting while their Southern counterparts in Upper Egypt cultivated food through agriculture.

Upper Egypt was symbolized by the Lotus and had 'White' kings while Lower Egypt was symbolized by the Papyrus and had 'Red' kings. And, for a long time, both lands where in endless conflict, never seeing eye to eye, as though they were polar opposites; so much so that when Egypt eventually became one the Pharaohs continued regarding themselves as 'Lords of two lands'. Whatever be the reason for the Egyptians' depth concerning the vitality of balance, the important takeaway here is that in most of their recently extracted art pieces, one would notice a perfect left side/right side equilibrium. A creatively designed pillar or wave of patterns, called a Sushumna, would run down the middle, and atop it would sit the Aten. It was easy to deduce that, for the Egyptians, the third eye was a confluence of energy and a force of balance. But even more than this, the Aten carried the double significance of being both the third eye and the 'soul within'; the thing that sees and the thing that is seen, at the same time. It was seen as a divine spark that awakened the soul to a higher self.

The third eye is like a light switch: it enables you seamlessly transcend levels of energy frequency within yourself. A higher level of spiritual energy is key to unlocking a higher consciousness and activating your extrasensory abilities. Opening your third eye can be viewed almost as self-acupuncture. By opening up your third eye, you automatically get in touch with a deeper aspect of your being, which in itself can have a very calming, almost therapeutic effect. Because of its nature as a psychic switch, the third eye also helps you manage several forms of energy and keep them flowing in the right direction.

Before we delve deeply into several techniques which will set you off strongly on the path to spiritual enlightenment and third eye awakening, we must touch on how you may handle the unique sensations which you may experience as you go further. Your third eye, otherwise called your Ajna chakra or pineal gland, is your portal to the divine realm. At the point when your third eye is open, you'll experience clear insight, receptiveness, scholarly parity, and a solid association with your instinct or internal shrewdness. Nonetheless, if your third eye is blocked or contracted, you'll battle with intolerance, overthinking, a sleeping disorder, choking out convictions, absence of direction, wretchedness, and a failure to interface with your Soul.

On the off chance that you need to feel associated with your inward reason and Soul's voice, probably the most ideal approaches to do that is by figuring out how to open your third eye.

AWAKEN YOUR EXTRASENSORY POWERS

At the point when the vast majority hear "extrasensory" they imagine mystics with gem balls foreseeing what's to come. In any case, I'm not alluding to this profoundly cliché picture when discussing extrasensory endowments. Rather, I characterize extrasensory blessings as the ability to get data past the ordinary five faculties of the body. As we probably are aware as of now, the body is essentially a vessel for Spirit; a manner by which we can see and decipher the physical realm. Yet, it is innocent to infer that the physical realm is all that exists as studies, for example, quantum material science and innumerable profound customs have instructed through the ages.

Extrasensory endowments are inalienable limits we have for "tuning into" different planes of presence, however most fundamentally, our own Souls. Furthermore, we as a whole have various limits. For instance, I have the endowment of clairaudience (clear hearing), clairsentience (clear feeling) and claircognizance (clear knowing) yet not special insight (clear seeing).

Here are the potential blessings you can open up to when you figure out how to open your third eye:

- Perceptiveness (clear seeing)
- Claircognizance (clear knowing)
- Clairaudience (clear hearing)
- Clairempathy (clear feeling)
- Clairtangency (clear knowing through touch)
- Clairsentience (clear knowing through feeling)

What's more, there are a couple of others, for example, clairgustance (in regard to taste) and clairsalience (with respect to smell).

The most significant thing isn't in waving around another name for yourself, yet the profound enhancement these blessings can give your life and your capacity to interface with, and comprehend, your Soul's astuteness.

STEP BY STEP INSTRUCTIONS TO OPEN YOUR THIRD EYE

Practically we all are naturally introduced to circumstances that urge our third eyes to close firmly. Since adolescence, we were shown an assortment of cultural, parental, strict thoughts and one-sided builds that cause us to get estranged from our internal knowledge.

Most eminently, we were urged to accommodate, comply with the guidelines, and overlook our inward voice, which now and again was even decried. In case you're battling to see existence with lucidity and feel confounded more often than not, you're likely overloaded with long periods of molding which instructed you to think and carry on with a particular goal in mind.

I realize firsthand how crippling and upsetting a shut third eye feels, and how it makes you vulnerable to being driven adrift.

HERE ARE MY TOP TIPS FOR FIGURING OUT HOW TO OPEN YOUR THIRD EYE

Move outside your usual range of familiarity and investigate elective convictions and thoughts. Shut third eyes blossom with extremism. Probably the most ideal approaches to open your psyche is to be mentally inquisitive.

Cutoff and ideally totally cut out handled nourishments. Our bodies were not intended to process the overflowing measures of fat, prepared starches, and sugars that are available in comfort and quick nourishments. You'll likewise profit by essentially diminishing your utilization of creature meats because of the hormones present in them.

Eat entire nourishments, vegetables, and organic products. Supplant the packeted nourishments you purchase with entire nourishments, for example, vegetables, nuts, entire grains, veggies, and organic products. Not exclusively do these leave you feeling more full, however they are more beneficial for your body and simpler for it to process. Your eating regimen is significant in light of the fact that it legitimately impacts your vitality levels, hormones, and along these lines feelings and musings.

Drink third eye purifying herbs. Herbs are a strong method to recalibrate your third eye. Attempt home grown teas that contain gotu kola, ginkgo biloba, rosemary, and passionflower. I suggest looking at Buddha Teas astonishing third eye Chakra Tea that is injected with the substance of sapphire.

Practice contemplation. Rather than attempting to control your contemplations and stances during reflection practice (like the vast majority do), essentially attempt to see what your psyche and body does.

The more mindful you become of your considerations, the more a space inside you opens.

Ground yourself through care. A significant indication of a useless third eye is overthinking. The most ideal approach to ground yourself right now is through a training known as care. Peruse progressively about care.

Stay away from fluoridated water and toothpaste. Studies have indicated that fluoride, the synthetic present in our drinking water and toothpaste, is liable for calcifying the pineal gland. At the point when your pineal gland becomes calcified, it stops to function admirably. Indeed, after a MRI examine, I found that my frontal flap is entirely calcified. Peruse increasingly about decalcifying the pineal gland.

Flood your body with cancer prevention agents. Cancer prevention agents are the superheroes of the nourishment world and are available in superfoods, for example, blueberries, goji berries, quinoa, maca, cacao, spirulina, coconuts, and numerous different foods grown from the ground. Cancer prevention agents detoxify and reinforce your body, which is ideal for figuring out how to open your third eye.

Investigate your center convictions. Your center convictions are oblivious thoughts you have about what your identity is and what you merit throughout everyday life. Center convictions keep you secured confining mentalities that keep your third eye shut. Figure out how to recognize your center convictions.

Exercise and drink loads of water. This is very obvious! Drinking water will likewise assist with flushing out the poisons in your body and hydrate your mind. (Simply attempt to maintain a strategic distance from fluoridated water!)

Diary and record your feelings. Perhaps the most ideal approaches to make lucidity and inward request is through recording how you feel. Do this every day and you'll encounter numerous psycho-profound advantages.

Murmur or serenade the sound "OM." Om is said to be the absolute first early stage sound of the universe, and conveys incredible vibrations that revive, rinse, and open your third eye.

Take a stab at making more blood and vitality course through yoga practice. Specifically, investigate the Balasana, Shavasana, and Dolphin present.

Investigate the old act of scrying. Scrying is an exclusive practice that encourages you to build up your inward vision. Peruse progressively about scrying.

Utilize sound recuperating. Sound conveys significantly mending vibrations. You can explore different avenues regarding instruments, for example, singing dishes, tuning forks, tolls, and chimes. These instruments vigorously orchestrate your third eye. Peruse progressively about sound recuperating instruments.

Do a third eye perception. Unwind, inhale profoundly, and envision a beating wad of purple light opening and clearing your third eye. Do this consistently for five minutes and focus on the manner in which you feel a short time later.

Investigate your subjective bends. We as a whole have subjective mutilations or mixed up convictions, and they tighten the progression of vitality through our third eye chakra. Perhaps the most ideal approaches to investigate your intellectual twists is by journaling about them. Find out about the most well-known mental snares.

Test with NLP. NLP or Neuro-linguistic programming encourages your psyche to move past constraining convictions and even fears that cause third eye visual impairment.

Practice care. Your third eye is the most open when it is grounded right now. Care is a training that can assist you with interfacing with the magnificence of the present time and place.

Utilize mending gems. Test with precious stones, for example, lapis lazuli, labradorite, sapphire, and kyanite. Utilize these precious stones in contemplation, perceptions, place them straightforwardly on your third eye, or convey them with you!

Bolster yourself through confirmations. Whatever you believe is the thing that you wind up showing. Attempt to adjust the manner in which you think and consequently invigorate third eye opening by attempting confirmations, for example, "I tune in to my internal astuteness," "I see with lucidity," "I confide in my instinct," "I trust in my capacities."

You'll likewise profit by daylight, isolation, and everyday pockets of quietness in your day. What Will Happen When My Third Eye Opens? When you've figured out how to open your third eye, you may be considering what the signs or side effects are. What would it be advisable for you to anticipate? Clearly, the experience shifts from individual to individual.

In any case, here are probably the most widely recognized signs that may happen gradually or suddenly:

- Shadow Work Journal
- Go on an excursion through the most profound and darkest corners of your mind. Grasp your inward evil presences, reveal your concealed blessings, and arrive at the following degree of your otherworldly development. This is profound and incredible work!
- Humming or shivering in your temple
- More cerebral pains or headaches than expected (your third eye is changing in accordance with the world)
- Dreams or extrasensory encounters during reflection
- Abrupt lucidity encompassing life issues
- Magical encounters
- Solid association with instinct and inward knowing
- Upgraded capacity to have an independent perspective
- There are numerous different indications, however these are the primary ones to pay special mind to.

Figuring out how to open your third eye takes commitment and the readiness to burrow profound and roll out a couple of improvements throughout your life. Be that as it may, the exertion you put in is well justified, despite all the trouble, and the endowment of lucidity will favor as long as you can remember for quite a long time to come.

When we start to practice meditation, it can look perplexing to come across the fact that there are numerous different procedures, we discovered this with the assistance of ta little list titled 'The Types of Meditation'. I first got this several years ago from Ruciraketu at the Oxford Buddhist Centre. I found it a valuable way then to comprehend the several meditation practices we might come across in our study of the dharma, and I'm giving it here as perhaps beneficial way for us to select the sort of practice for us at any given time.

Having said that, we also wish to aim to grow in consciousness and kindness in a composed and rounded way, and whereas we might choose to concentrate on one or the other of these, I'd propose we need all of them to be existing as measure of real spiritual practice! Whether you're fascinated with meditation or just inquisitive about what it is, you might find yourself coming across several diverse practices. The term "meditation" incorporates practices from several different civilizations, religions, and modalities. We've made all effort to refer to a few of the common forms of meditation, concentrating mostly on the kinds of meditation in Buddhism.

There are meditation practices that are not Buddhist in nature, and we will talk about those a bit as well. Conversely, our personal knowledge comes primarily from Buddhist traditions. We've separated the practices out into Buddhist meditation methods, movement practices, and meditation methods from other sources.

1. Concentrative: There is a body of practices whose objective is to still the mind, to gather us together when we are isolated, to assist us to focus and be present whenever we are preoccupied and 'allover the place'. Mindfulness practices such as the Mindfulness of Breathing are a standard practice for this goal.

2. Generative: This is the body of practices that assist us grow and develop more of a quality that we hope to have more present in our life - compassion, generosity, elation in others for instance. The foundation for these practices is that we could train ourselves to have more of these potentials - like building up a muscle through exercise. The Growth of Loving Kindness (Metta Bhavana) is a vital practice here.

3. Receptive: This is a important skill to acquire - to be totally open and able to turn towards our real experience, beyond and beneath our layers of cultural habituation that make us blindly agree to take assumptions of 'how things are'. The practice at this point is what we call in Triratna Just Sitting.

4. Reflective: learning to think - in a calm, focused, directed way, permitting us to go deeper and discover our exact and truly creative way of linking to the globe - the capability to do this very much hinge on some grounding in the above three skills.

I am just adding the poem by James Keyes 'Hokusei says' as we read it at the conclusion of the class and it is one of

I. MINDFULNESS MEDITATION

Mindfulness meditation is perhaps what you think about whenever you ponder on Buddhist meditation. In mindfulness meditation, we rest in a enduring awareness, tuning into our experience with acknowledgement and present-time thoughtfulness. The aim of meditation with mindfulness is to get understanding into the nature of reality. Exactly, we are to note the Three Marks of Existence: dukkha, non-self, and temporariness. Though here are a few precise methods used to nurture mindfulness traditionally.

Body Scanning: A body scan meditation is always one of the first methods person find. It's make use in secular settings, Buddhist groups, and yoga lessons at times. In a body scan you course through the body gradually, paying attention meticulously to each part of the body and feelings present. It could be done seated or lying down, and you could come back to the practice in day-to-day life.

This type of meditation is a valuable technique for novices as it keeps the mind slightly engaged with changing stimulation. The body scan practice aids you to bring mindfulness to what is arising and passing in the body, knowing your individual present-time experience.

Mindfulness of Breath: is actually as it sounds: a form of meditation in which you practice consciousness of the breathing. It is always practiced from the guiding principle of the Anapanasati Sutta, or discourse on instituting mindfulness of the breath. In this form of mindfulness meditation, you are using the breath in the body as the purpose of your awareness.

This is another type of meditation that several folks come to know pretty quick in their meditation pathway. Concentrating on the breath is a normal practice used in secular settings and outside Buddhist contemplation groups, and it is beneficial in daily life and any condition. It's vital to comprehend there is a variance between mindfulness of breath and attentiveness practice, which we will cover in a bit.

Open Awareness: is a sort of mindfulness in which you relax in a patient state of waiting for something to ascend in your experience. It is a little less organized than a body scan or mindfulness of the breath and might be more challenging for those new to meditation. Moreover, this is the kind of meditation that really assists to nurture the skill of mindfulness and acknowledgement.

You could begin an era of open awareness with some mindfulness of breathing or a body scan, though you will open your awareness up to grasp what else is arising. Observe the feelings, sounds, aromas, tastes, feelings in the body, and sights. You observe the responses and rejoinders of the mind, the liking and abhorring of experiences, and the ephemeral nature of experience.

Vipassana: is a practice that is understood to have come from the Buddha himself, and has gotten admiration in the West in the last century with S.N. Goenka and his vipassana centers. Vipassana practices begin with concentrating on the breath, most frequently at the tip of the nose or inside the nostrils. Ultimately, you open up to other experiences ascending and passing, returning to the feeling of the body breathing.

Where vipassana turn into a special type of meditation is in the noting. Mental noting is the exercise of saying to yourself in your head what is arising or transient. If you witness a sound, you note "audible range." If you identify a thought is present, you note "rational." It might look intricate, though I for my part use this practice daily. It's extremely useful, and you will get the hang of it by actually trying it!

2. LOVING-KINDNESS MEDITATION

However, we have Metta. Metta is a Pali word that is always interpreted as loving-kindness or gentle friendliness. It is one of the customary heart practices in Buddhism, and is the nurturing of a generous, gentle, and caring heart. You could think of Metta as the modest quality of wishing well for others (and yourself) in your life. This is done via a practice termed loving-kindness meditation. There are several ways to nurture loving-kindness, however, the most common is done through the repetition of phrases. A sort of Samatha meditation, this calms the mind, concentrate our intentions, and gradually opens the heart to care for beings.

3. COMPASSION MEDITATION

Compassion is just another of the heart practices, and the actual procedure is comparable to Metta. This is a procedure I constantly introduce to beginners, as it is beneficial to address our relationship to hitches and judgement from the start. Additionally, compassion meditation actually works,

In compassion meditation, you could use phrases to develop a mind and heart that can tend to the moments of discomfort and exertion with care. You could think of compassion as what occurs when loving-kindness comes into contact with misery. It's a type of meditation that could assist us in practice when challenging moments arise, and in our daily lives as we face difficulties and pains.

4. GRATEFUL JOY

The next type of meditation is an additional heart method. called Mudita, this is what occurs when Metta comes into contact with elation and cheerfulness. We foster the capability to celebrate in the happiness of others and appreciate the happiness in life. Rather than falling into resentment or judgement, we open the heart to carefully take in the gladness others experience.

This again is done via the repetition of phrases and concentrated attention. As with other heart meditations, you might not always feel loving and kind while doing it. Moreover, you continue to practice, cultivating this intent to open the heart. These procedures that use phrases are not a quick fix (no sort of meditation is), and it takes time.

5. CALMNESS PRACTICE

The last heart practice we have is equanimity. Equanimity is the worth of mind and heart which remain stable, particularly when presented with emotive or strong experiences. With equanimity, we stay mindful and present, and don't get knocked off balance. This takes nurturing, though over time we are capable of meeting experiences with a patient wisdom.

In equability meditation, we use phrases to know our own power to select how we meet experiences. Rather than trying to control others or outside situations, we identify that we have imperfect control.

6. CONCENTRATION MEDITATION

Going away from the heart practices, we're going to cover a few other methods to contemplate that come from Buddhist roots. Concentration is a practice rooted extremely in the Buddhist traditions, as the Buddha himself sat in concentration quite regularly (according to suttas). In case the name doesn't make it apparent, this is a kind of meditation in which we cultivate the capability to concentrate.

There are several diverse ways to practice attentiveness meditation, though the most common is by concentrating on the breath in one point in the body. Whenever the mind wanders, you bring it forth. It takes lots of time to build concentration, moreover each time you ponder you are consolidating on the mental muscle. You could also build concentration working with sounds, phrases of Metta, or any other object of consciousness.

7. ZAZEN

As stated, there are many different forms of meditation practice. Theravada and Mahayana Buddhism have special methods, and this is one of them. Zazen is of the Zen tradition, and is a practice that is reliant upon studying (as all meditation truly should be). In zazen meditation, you emphasis on the breath and permit thoughts to come and go. They will decrease naturally.

Though this practice is very comparable to concentration practices of other traditions, zazen is a bit more organized. Different traditions have definite postures, mudras of the hands, and means to practice. You might get guidelines to sit with eyes open, to breathe via the mouth, or to count the breaths.

8. CHANTING PRACTICES

There are chanting meditations in several diverse traditions. In some customs, like Pure Land Buddhism, a definite mantra is chanted continually. In some others, sacred texts are recited together by followers. Chanting gives a form of present-time attentiveness that uses hearing, speaking, and feeling in the body. It is another means to develop intention and be present. You could get chanting in Nichiren Buddhism, Pure Land Buddhism, some types of Theravada Buddhism, and many Tibetan practices. This is actually not a method of meditation I rehearse, other than my time on retreat and at monasteries.

9. TONGLEN

Tonglen meditation originates from the Tibetan tradition of meditation. It's a kind of meditation that aids us see with empathy and let go of our own problems. By tradition, you breathe in the despondency and darkness from the world around you and give out your wishes of love and kindness. You identify that others are distress, maybe in a similar way as you.

In the West, some instructors also reverse this practice a bit. You could breathe in well-wishes for yourself, at that moment let go of the unpleasant as you breathe out. Moreover, the practice of Tonglen is all about sharing and getting. Customarily, we are nurturing a heart that cares for the pain and misery in the world and meeting it with our own kindhearted care.

All of the techniques to meditate we've covered have been practices of sitting meditation. Even though, this is what you possibly think of when you think of meditation, there are actually several customary ways to practice even though moving the body. Moving meditation gives a way to meditate in a novel posture and in a innovative way. I strongly suggest integrating a movement practice into your normal meditation practice.

1. WALKING MEDITATION

Walking meditation is an essential practice in Buddhism and numerous other traditions. Similar to sitting meditation, you concentrate on the mind on an object and observe when the mind rambles. The only change is that your body is moving. You might concentrate on the breath, on phrases of loving-kindness, or on the responsiveness of the body moving in space. Walking meditation might look silly or futile, though it is an integral practice for numerous Buddhists across the globe. Monks and nuns frequently rehearse walking meditation at monasteries, and you would find periods of walking meditation on numerous retreats. Beneath is a moderately short walking practice you could try to familiarize yourself to how it's done.

2. KUNDALINI

There are several forms of yoga meditation, and yoga might be seen generally as a meditation practice itself. Nevertheless, we're going to cover one of the more conventionally meditative practices: kundalini. Kundalini meditation is the practice of arousing the kundalini energy in the base of the spine. This is entrenched in Hinduism, and the emphasis is on bringing the energy up by means of the seven chakras.

I honestly don't know a whole lot about this form of meditation, though I wanted to give it in our list since I have tried it earlier and found it beneficial. Moreover, I know when folks ask us about kinds of meditation, kundalini is one that looks to pop up to a certain extent. You could check out kundalini meditations on YouTube or Insight Timer for some tutoring!

3. QIGONG

Qigong is an olden practice coming from Chinese wisdom and medicine. With the purpose of conserving strength and balancing energy, qigong could be an intensely meditative practice. Whenever, I stay at Deer Park Monastery, I'm at all times thankful for the eras of qigong. Like yoga, you have the chance to be conscious of your body and energies when moving rather than sitting still. You could take an online qigong course or go on YouTube to get started

4. TAI CHI

Tai chi is an additional Chinese practice, though more of a martial art. Even though it was traditionally a kind of the martial arts, it has become a common kind of meditation while moving. According to Harvard Health, tai chi has several health benefits both physically and spiritually.

As with several of the other meditation kinds on our list, I don't know enough to give recommendations or guidelines for starting the practice. Conversely, I have heard from individuals who do practice that an in-person class is certainly the way to go! You can also get YouTube videos online giving lessons.

Furthermore, we have some other meditation methods. Some of these are used in numerous traditions, some are nonspiritual, and some are just separate practices. You could examine the practices for yourself to see what is beneficial.

1. FORGIVENESS MEDITATION

Forgiveness meditation is regularly incorporated in Buddhist circles and groups, although is not a customary heart practice. Like the other heart practices, you could use phrases to nurture a mind and heart inclined in the direction of forgiving. Instructors like Jack Kornfield and Sharon Salzberg inspire forgiveness practice, and I've found it to be intensely beneficial in working with the judgements and dislikes. Forgiveness takes time, and we might not be ready to exonerate in this moment. We continue to encourage a slow opening and permit ourselves to journey along the path rather than requiring for instant forgiveness.

2. TRANSCENDENTAL MEDITATION

Transcendental Meditation is a relatively new method, presented in the 1950's by Maharishi Mahesh Yogi. In Transcendental Meditation, you practice by restating a mantra for stages of 22 minutes, two times a day. You take your mantra and training by joining a course, which is communicated in a series of seven phases. Transcendental Meditation became specifically prevalent in the 1970's as numerous celebrities started practicing. Moreover, a lot of the research on meditation centers on this sort of practice. Though it's different than many Buddhist sorts of meditation, it might be seen as a sort of concentration practice.

3. VISUALIZATION PRACTICES

There are too numerous visualization practices to cover here. In visualization practices, you are making use of the power of the mind to bring forward a condition, scenario, or experience to work with. Many types of non-religious meditation make use visualization practices to assist manifest consequences and needs. Whether you're imagining a past experience that was difficult or your dream vacation in Panama and taking a trip to Playa del Carmen, visualization makes a way to bring up detailed experiences.

There are also visualization practices giving by psychotherapists and Buddhist meditation instructors. Tara Brach is a delightful example, using visualization practices with her Metta and compassion practices to assist in stimulating the mind and precise emotions. It's a method that works particularly well for persons who think visually. You could find Tara's meditations on her YouTube channel, where some give visualization in the meditation.

4. MEDITATING ON GOD

Conversely, there are numerous forms of meditation that center on a connection with a god or higher power. This comprises spiritual meditations, Christian meditations, Buddhist meditations, and lots more. In these practices, you will concentrate on the presence of a god or divinity, ask for assistance, or practice listening. Though this is something I don't generally do, I know several members of our greater sangha who benefit significantly from these practices.

BENEFITS OF DIFFERENT TECHNIQUES

Thanks to years and years of study, we are starting to comprehend the advantages of meditation. Each sort of meditation gives different ways to support you in your life, comprising the capability to decrease stress, advance mental health, and take care of the physical body. Moving practices are of course good for the body, and concentration practices noticeably could assist in building concentration. Nevertheless, there are some advantages of different kinds of meditation which are not so noticeable. For instance, mindfulness meditation can support depression, anxiety, sleep disorders, and other difficulties with mental health. Concentration practice might lower heart rate and blood pressure, or even decrease stress overall. A study in 2010 found that thoughtful prayer and yoga enhanced symptoms of premenstrual syndrome and menopause. Each type of meditation gives a different type of benefits. Heart practices open the heart, however, also assist to figure out concentration. Mindfulness supports building present-time consciousness, though could also reduce anger. When you jump into choosing a technique for yourself, you may consider which practice calls out to you to help relieve some suffering.

CHAPTER 4: DISCOVERING THE RIGHT METHOD FOR YOURSELF

With all of the choices and different methods, it could be tough to pick just one. The good news is that you don't principally have to! You could try diverse methods for a well-rounded and complete practice, or at least explore different ones to see what is valuable.Before going into each and every kind on this list, I suggest starting with a technique that aids you build some attentiveness and socializing in some eras of Metta or compassion. Beginning like this, you could cultivate the capability to focus in the course meditation and reply with patience when the mind doesn't behave precisely how you wish it to. As you continue to practice, you will get yourself able to sit longer and pay close attention with less interruption. From here, you could move on and start considering other kinds of meditation. Don't bother yourself too much. If you try each and every kind, you might be left without uniformity. Select a technique and stay with it for a bit before moving on. If you're fascinated in starting a practice, however, don't know where to start, you could reach out to one of our mindfulness coaches to get some assistance!

MINDFULNESS MEDITATION

ORIGIN & MEANING

Mindfulness Meditation is a reworking from usual Buddhist meditation practices, precisely Vipassana, on the other hand having strong impact from other lineages (like the Vietnamese Zen Buddhism from Thich Nhat Hanh). "Mindfulness" is the standard western explanation for the Buddhist expression sati. Anapanasati, "mindfulness of breathing", is chunk of the Buddhist practice of Vipassana or intuition meditation, and other Buddhist meditational practices, like zazen One of the foremost influencers for Mindfulness in the West is John Kabat-Zinn. His Mindfulness-Based Stress Reduction package (MBSR) – which he started in 1980 at the University of Massachusetts Medical School – has been used in numerous hospitals and health clinic in the past years.

Mindfulness meditation is the practice of intentionally concentrating on the present moment, accepting and non-judgmentally paying attention to the feelings, thoughts, and emotions that arise. For the "proper practice" time, sit down on a cushion on the floor, or on a chair, with straight and unsupported back. Pay close attention to the drive of your breath. Whenever you breath in, be aware that you are breathing in, and how it senses. Whenever you breath out, be mindful you are breathing out. Do like this for the duration of your meditation practice, constantly redirecting the attention to the breath. Or you could move on to be paying close attention to the sensations, opinions and feelings that come up.The effort is to not purposely add anything to our present moment experience, yet to be conscious of what is going on, without losing ourselves in whatsoever that get up.

Your mind will get engrossed into going along with sounds, sensations, and thoughts. Whenever that ensues, gently know that you have been distracted, and bring the consideration back to the breathing, or to the objective observing of that thought or sensation. There is a huge different between being in the thought/sensation, and simply being conscious of it's existence.

Learn to appreciate your practice. As soon as you are done, appreciate how diverse the body and mind sense. There is also the practice of mindfulness in our daily undertakings: even though consuming, walking, and talking. For "daily life" reflection, the practice is to pay attention to what is going on in the current moment, to be conscious of what is trendy – and not living in "instinctive mode".

If you are speaking, that means paying attention to the words you communicate, how you express them, and to listen with presence and rap attention. When you are walking, that means being more conscious of your body movements, your feet touching the ground, the echoes you are hearing, etc. Your exertion in seated practice helps your daily life practice, and vice-versa. They are both similarly significant.

For the general public, this is possibly the most sensible way to get going with meditation. It is the kind of meditation that is most learned at schools and hospitals, as far as I am aware. The "mindfulness movement" as practiced these days in society at large, is not Buddhism, though an adaptation of Buddhist practices because of their advantages in good physical and mental health and general wellbeing.

For most persons, Mindfulness Meditation might be the only form of meditation they will like, particularly if their concentration is merely the physical and mental benefits of meditation, as it is regularly taught disconnected from some of the eastern concepts and philosophies that traditionally complemented the practice. And for that it is exceptional – it will bring numerous worthy things to your life. If your focus is a deeper transformation and spiritual development, moreover, then mindfulness meditation might be just an initial step for you. From here you could then go into Vipassana, Zazen, or other forms of meditation.

LOVING KINDNESS MEDITATION (METTA MEDITATION)

ORIGIN & MEANING

Metta is a Pali word that connotes compassion, generosity, and good will. This practice originates from the Buddhist traditions, particularly the Theravada and Tibetan roots. "Compassion meditation" is a contemporary scientific field that launches the effectiveness of metta and related meditative practices.

Demonstrated benefits consist of: improving one's capability to sympathize with others; development of positive emotions via compassion, comprising a more loving attitude concerning oneself; improved self-acceptance; greater feeling of capability about one's life; and increased feeling of resolve in life.

HOW TO DO IT

One will sits down in a meditation spot, with closed eyes, and produces in his mind and heart spirits of kindness and compassion. Begin by evolving loving-kindness concerning yourself, then increasingly towards others and all beings. Typically this development is advised:

- Oneself
- A virtuous friend
- A "neutral" person
- A problematic person
- All four of the above likewise
- And then slowly the whole universe

The feeling to be advanced is that of coveting happiness and well-being for all. This practice might be helped by rehearsing exact words or sentences that arouse the "boundless warm-hearted feeling", visualizing the suffering of others and sending love; or by picturing the state of another being, and wishing him contentment and peace. The more you practice this meditation, the more happiness you will experience. That is the top-secret of Mathieu Richard's happiness.

There is not one kind of meditation which is "Yogic Meditation", Thus here it is meant the several meditation kinds taught in the yoga custom. Yoga means "union". The Custom goes as far as 1700 B.C. and has as its topmost goal spiritual cleansing and Self-Knowledge. Classical Yoga splits the practice into guidelines of conduct (Yamas and Niyamas), physical postures (Asanas), breathing workouts (Pranayama), and meditative practices of meditation (Pratyahara, Dharana, Dhyana, Samadhi).

The Yoga custom is the ancient meditation practice on earth, and also the one with the extensive variety of practices.

These are some kinds of meditation practiced in Yoga. The most popular and general Yoga meditation one is the "third eye meditation". Other prevalent ones consist of concentrating on a chakra, reiterating a mantra, visualization of light, or staring meditations.

Third Eye Meditation — centering the attention on the "spot amid the eyebrows" (termed by some "the third eye" or "ajna chakra"). The attention is continually redirected to this position, as a way to calm the mind. By the time the "silent openings" amid thoughts get wider and deeper. Sometimes this is complemented by physically "looking", with eyes shut, in the direction of that spot.

Chakra Meditation — the specialist concentrates on one of the seven chakras of the body ("core of energy"), usually doing some visualizations and invoking a precise mantra for each chakra (lam, vam, ram, yam, ham, om). Most usually it is done on the heart chackra, third eye, and crown chackra.

Gazing Meditation (Trataka) — protecting the stare on an external object, characteristically a rush candle, image or a symbol (yantras). It is gotten with eyes open, and however with eyes closed, to train both the attentiveness and imagining powers of the mind. Subsequently closing the eyes, you ought to still retain the image of the object in your "mind's eye". This meditation is so key and dominant,

Kundalini Meditation — this is a very multifaceted method of practice. The objective is the growing of the "kundalini energy" which lies inactive on the base of the spine, the growth of numerous psychic centers in the body, and, ultimately, explanation. There are numerous risks connected with this practice, and it should not be tried devoid of the guidance of a competent yogi.

Kriya Yoga — is a set of energization, aware, and meditation exercises educated by Paramahamsa Yogananda. This is more suitable for those who have a sacred character, and are looking for the spiritual aspects of meditation. To learn more, you could apply to get the Self-Realization lessons,

Sound Meditation (**Nada Yoga**) — concentrating on sound. Begins with meditation on "exterior sounds", like reassuring ambient music (like Native American flute music), where the student concentration all his attention on mere hearing, as an assist to allay and collect the mind. By time the practice advances to hearing the "internal sounds" of the body and mind. The final objective is to hear the "Critical Sound" (para nada), which is a sound deprived of vibration, and that displays as "OM".

Tantra — Due to the prevalent opinion in the West, most Tantra practices have nothing to do with ritualized sex (this was taught by a minority of lineages. Tantra is a very rich tradition, with loads of different meditative practices. The text Vijnanabhairava Tantra, for example, lists 109 "meditations", most of them more innovative (already needing some certain degree of stillness and mind control). These are some examples from that text:

- Combine the mind and the senses in the interior space in the mystical heart.
- When one object is observed, all other objects become blank. Focus on that emptiness.
- Focus on the space which happens between two thoughts.

- Fix consideration on the inside of the skull. Close eyes.
- Meditate at the instance of any great delight.
- Reflect on the feeling of pain.
- Dwell on the certainty which subsists between pain and pleasure.
- Meditate on the void in one's body spreading in all directions instantaneously.
- Focus on a never-ending well or as standing in a very high place.
- Pin your ears on the Anahata [heart chakra] sound.
- Eavesdrop on the sound of a musical instrument as it passes away away.
- Ponder on the globe or one's own body as being filled with ecstasy.
- Deliberate passionately on the notion that the universe is entirely void.
- Consider that the same mindfulness exists in all bodies.

Pranayama — breathing regulation. It is not precisely meditation, though a brilliant practice to calm the mind and get ready for meditation. There are numerous different sorts of Pranayama, however the simplest and most normally taught one is the 5-5-5-5. This connotes breathing in counting up to 5 holding for 5 seconds, breathing out for 5 seconds, and holding empty for 5 seconds. Breathe by means of your nose and permit the abdomen (and not the chest) be the one that moves. Go through a few cycles such as this. This regulation of breathing stabilizes the moods and appeases the body and could be done anywhere. Yoga is indeed a rich tradition, with diverse lineages, hence there are lots of other procedures. Though the ones above are the most celebrated; the others are more detailed or composite.

CHAPTER 5: A REAL CONNECTION BETWEEN YOUR BODY AND MEDITATION

For the purpose of full disclosure, I should state that I don't like the terms "mind-body connection" and "mind-body medication" too much. From what I've perceived, most persons who make use of the phrase "mind-body" look to mean the way your mind, principally your feelings, can impact the functioning of the body. Though that notion might have once looked radical, to the yogi it's much clear. In yoga, moreover, we recognize that this aspect of the mind-body association is actually only slice of the story.

I've overheard yoga instructors state the mind-body connection as something obscure, a connection we anticipate to copy with our yoga practice. In truth, the mind-body connection is prevailing all the time—for better and worse—whether we or our learners are conscious of it or not. Contemplate a few instances.

If your mouth waters at the assumed of a dish you cherish, you're feeling the mind-body connection. If you've constantly touched the butterflies in the pit of your stomach as you are ready to make a presentation, you've sensed how your thoughts affect the operation of your intestines. An athlete who "chokes" at a big instant in a competition, acting worse than normal, is correspondingly seeing the consequences of an appalling state of mind on his or her capability to organize muscular actions.

Experiencing the mind-body connection is a routine happening, not something that only the forward-looking yogi can attain. The problem—and the purpose we've got the idea of mind-body medicine at all—is that frequently the connection is all too real, and it causes complications. You might have students who are so nervous or tense   that they can't sleep well or focus on their work. Others might be carrying around so much fury that they're setting themselves up for bleeding ulcers or heart attacks.

What we are doing when we teach our students skills like pratyahara (the turning of the minds inward) and Dhyana (meditation) is truly getting their minds out of the way. Without the meddling of their normal nervous or annoyed thoughts, the stress response system reduces, and the body can do a better work of curing itself. You could state that, in a moment, that mind-body medicine works by breaking the mind-body connection, at least for a little while.

At Harvard Medical School's Mind-Body Medical Institute, Dr. Herbert Benson and contemporaries teach a method they name the Relaxation Response, which is a clarified system of meditation, modeled straight on Transcendental Meditation (TM), a kind of yogic mantra contemplation. Many studies have shown that when you silence the mind with these procedures, a range of useful physiological responses—comprising lessen heart rate, breathing rate, blood pressure, and levels of stress hormones—outcome, benefiting situations from migraines to high blood pressure to barrenness.

Although most yogic practices have not been taught as much as TM and the Relaxation Response, it makes sense that wide collection of yogic tools, from incantation to Pranayama practices like Ujjayi (Triumphant Breath) and Bhramari (Buzzing Bee Breath) to other meditation procedures, all of which foster pratyahara and silent the mind, would have comparable health benefits. And several yogis have the believe that there are additive benefits from merging different practices—for instance, by doing pranayama as a run-up to meditation.

THE BODY-MIND CONNECTION

WAYS YOUR BODY UPSETS YOUR MIND

The piece that I occasionally find lost in deliberations of mind-body medicine, moreover, this is the technique that your body could affect the state of your mind. This again comes as no amazement to the yogi, nor to anyone else who is paying close attention. Most persons have discovered that working out, whether it's going for a walk or doing an energetic yoga class, could lift their mood. A massage or a hot bath can get rid of stress. It works the other way too: Consistent exercisers might observe themselves feeling cranky if they are deprived of their typical physical outlet numerous days in a row.

Physical illness could also have nonstop effects on your mental point of view. On numerous times over the years, I have found myself feeling dejected for no reason I could control. Simply the next morning, when a sore throat, nasal congestion, and other flu signs had emerged, did I recognize that my sour mood had been the way my mind was responding to the imminent illness (and my body's reply to it), although I had no conscious alertness of it. You could call this piece of the mystery the body-mind connection.

"Take a deep breath," the simple injunction usually given when someone is annoyed or stressed out, is the acceptance of the body-mind connection. And this is, of course, the standard that we are taking benefit of in asana practice in particular. Yogis have known that definite poses, such as backbends and side stretches, used to be inspiring to the mind, while others, just like forward bends and inversions, have a tendency to encourage a quieter, more thoughtful state.

WHAT IS THE MIND-BODY CONNECTION?

Cultured, slim, and good-looking, Julie appears to have it all. She has a PhD, an exciting career, and good support system. So, everything's great, right? Not precisely. Juliet also has diabetes. And while she adore her job, she feels nervous about running a business. She always gets livid with herself, and shouts at others for small mistakes. Even terrifying, in spite of careful watching of her blood sugar, she finds herself in a coma once or two times a month. What's going on?

It turns out that in spite of Julie usually healthy practices, her anxiety stops her from paying attention to the signs her body gives her whenever her blood sugar is too low.

On her medic's advice, Julie attempts Mindfulness Based Stress-Reduction (MBSR) classes along with her consistent diabetes care program. The MBSR practices assist Sylvia slow down and truly pay close attention to her body. Julie starts to notice when her blood sugar is reducing, so she could eat to stop herself from going into a diabetic coma. She also discovers it stress-free to regulate her diabetes with insulin, perhaps because decreasing her anxiety helps lower her stress hormones. Her frustration, a product of her stress, also die away.

WHAT IS THE MIND-BODY CONNECTION?

Julie's story is a great case in point of what we call the mind-body connection. This says that our thoughts, emotional state, beliefs, and attitudes can absolutely or adversely affect our biological functioning. Moreover, our minds could disturb how healthy our bodies are! In addition, what we do with our physical body (what we ingest, how much we workout, even our posture) can influence our mental state (again certainly or negatively). This leads to a complex interrelationship between our minds and bodies "the brain and peripheral nervous system, the endocrine and immune systems, and undoubtedly, all the tissues of our body and all the emotional responses we have, give a correct chemical language and are continuously communicating with one another." Dr. James gardener (originator of the Center for Mind-Body Medicine)

WHAT ARE BODY-MIND THERAPIES?

Related to mind-body therapies are therapies that make use of the body to upset the mind, like yoga, tai chi, qigong, and some forms of dance (these are sometimes known as body-mind therapies). In the long run mind-body and body-mind therapies are interconnected: the body have emotional impact on the mind, which in turn controls the body (and the mind.)

- Patient support groups
- Cognitive-behavioral therapy
- Meditation
- Prayer
- Creative arts therapies (art, music, or dance)
- Yoga
- Biofeedback
- Tai chi
- Qigong
- Relaxation
- Hypnosis
- Guided imagery

WHAT PRECISELY IS MEANT BY THE EXPRESSION "MIND?"

It's essential to note that "mind" is not identical to the brain. Instead, in our meaning, the mind comprises of mental states like thoughts, feelings, beliefs, attitudes, and images. The brain is the hardware that permits us to experience these mental situations. Mental states could be completely conscious or unconscious. We could have emotional reactions to conditions without being conscious of why we are responding.

Each mental state has a physiology connected with it—a positive or negative effect felt in the physical body. For instance, the mental state of anxiety causes you to manufacture stress hormone s. Several mind-body therapies concentrate on becoming more mindful of mental states and using this improved awareness to direct our mental states in an improved, less vicious direction.

WHAT IS THE HISTORY OF MIND-BODY CONNECTION?

Attentiveness of the mind-body connection is by no means novel. Until roughly 3oo years ago, nearly every system of medicine all through the world treated the mind and body as complete. Though all through the 18th century, the Western world began to see the mind and body as two separate entities. In this assessment, the body was sort of like a machine, complete with consumable, independent parts, with no connection of any kind to the mind.

This Western standpoint had certain benefits, stand-in as the foundation for developments in surgery, trauma care, pharmaceuticals, and other regions of allopathic medicine. Moreover, it also greatly lessens scientific investigation into humans' emotional and spiritual life and moderated their innate capability to heal.

In the 2oth century, this view began to change. Scholars began to learn the mind-body connection and precisely establish multifaceted links between the body and mind. Integrative psychiatrist James Arnold MD, of Stanford University States that "extensive research has proven the medical and mental advantages of contemplation, mindfulness training, yoga, and other mind-body practices." Everyday stress and problems in life could lead to protracted illness. This is because your mind and body are linked in a thoughtful way. By taking care of your body via exercise and diet, you would be better-off.

To maintain the body in good health is a duty...else we should not be able to keep our mind robust and unblemished.

Buddha said "Your **body is your temple, and you merely get one in this generation. You should wake up every day knowing that you are going to take care it via exercise and proper fuel."** (Most of the time).

Whenever you do, you will also recognize that your mind is unblemished, creative, and positive and that you are contented. This medical spectacle is the mind + body connection. Your moods, emotions state, stress-levels, and events in your daily life do influence your health.

A Parent's Normal Day:

- 5:3o am – alarm goes off, eat, bath, get kitted
- 6:3o am– get the children up, get them well served and well dressed
- 7:3o am– out the door, drop the children off at school
- 8:3o am– you could to the office barraged with questions, phone calls, via e-mail
- You work your barrel off all day and eat lunch at your desk.
- 4:4o pm– leave for work and maybe put in that workout
- 5:3o pm– pick the children up
- 6:3o pm – dinner is prepared and served, or you are at some kind of children sports practice

Next 3 hours: Wash the dishes, bathe and prepare children for bed, break up child fights, take the children to bed

10:3o pm – Get yourself on bed since you only get 6 hours of sleep if you fall asleep RIGHT AWAY!! It was only Monday...You would have to do this all over again every day for the rest of the week, and it's draining and traumatic. Does this sound all too acquainted? It prepares me too.

Demanding daily routines combined with not taking care of your body could lead to severe health concerns.

THE MIND & BODY CONNECTION

There is a deep connection concerning your emotional health and your bodily health. When your emotions are running on high, your body senses the stress and responds to it.

For example, think of a particularly stressful day on the job. You may have sat in your chair all day dealing with issues and problems, but when you left work you felt physically drained, almost as if you had run a marathon. This is your body's reaction to stress.

This can also happen when other situations arise such as:

- Job loss
- Starting a new job
- Birth of a child
- Death in the family
- Divorce
- Caring for an elderly parent
- Boredom
- Financial strain

And the list goes on...

HISTORY OF MIND & BODY CONNECTION

A Medical journal states that till the 1820s doctors believed that emotions were linked to disease. They would recommend "holidays" to sea-side resorts and other relaxation dwellings. Don't you wish those were still prescribed today?

The theory was that by monitoring the emotions and keeping them in a sound state that the body would follow in health. As medicine became more forward-thinking and scientific discoveries were recounting at a fast pace, the mind-body connection was abandoned, till lately. In the past three decades or so the mind-body connection has been reexamined. Studies have shown connections concerning emotional and physical health. The Center for Mind Body Medicine stated that up to 85% of all illnesses are connected to protracted stress.

Mind-body medicine, frequently referred to as complementary and alternative medicine, or CAM, has been put into place to ease stress and prolonged illness. What are some of the types of mind-body medicine? According to The US Department of Health and Human Resources, the most common forms of mind-body medicine are these four:

- Yoga
- Meditation
- Tai chi
- Hypnosis

Finding Your Exercise Outlet. I definitely have confidence in it, we could use other methods of exercise as mind-body medicine. For example, some folks love running. It is therapeutic for them. It aids some persons to clear their minds after a busy day and ease stress which is what other types of alternative medicine do for you.

What's imperative is that you find a form of exercise that you relish whether it's Zumba, weights lifting, playing tennis, or martial arts. Whenever you find an activity you adore, you are more probable to make it routine. Your new routine will have a healthy impression on your body and your mind. It might be hard at first, though I have never met anyone who ended a workout and said, "Oh, I wish I had not worked out today!"

Current Body-State of Americans. America is certainly losing the battle of the bulge. The Centers for Disease Control and Prevention states that roughly 37% of American adults are obese. Obesity could lead to depression, high blood pressure, diabetes, some cancers and other protracted illnesses. Folks instantly resort to prescription medications to "fix" their illnesses in place of altering their mind + body connections.

WHAT DO I MEAN BY CHANGING THEIR MIND & BODY CONNECTION?

What I'm talking about is a routine change. Initially, take care of your body. The "cure" should not have to be prescription medicines. A true fix would be to begin exercising again; walk every evening with you kids or pets or both. Why? Endorphins. The American Psychological Association states that exercise has both short- and long-term advantages. They cited Michael Otto, PhD, a professor of psychology at Michigan University, who declared that, "The link between exercise and mood is very strong. Habitually within six minutes after adequate exercise you get a mood-enhancement outcome."

This is because whenever we exercise, our brains discharge endorphins that improve our mood. Experts states that endorphins intermingle with receptors in your brain and actually lessen your perception of pain. Endorphins also prompt a happy feeling comparable to the feeling caused by the use of morphine. As you could see, our bodies and minds have an essential and dominant connection with one another.

When you are feeling worried, depressed, and the challenges of life are piling up on you, recall that your stress will have a negative effect on your body, it's effective, and its health. Turn to day-to-day reprieve in the form of exercise. Discover and form of exercise that you relish and look forward to. Not only will you appease your mind, though you will soothe your body and bring back your health. Your mind + body connection is the robust connection that you have total control over.

For centuries, healers have considered the connection between mental and physical health. In recent years, science has started to recognize the prevailing connections through which responsive, spiritual, and behavioral factors can instantly affect health consequences.

Emotions and thought configurations could led to inequalities in the body, and therapies like hypnosis, visual imagery, meditation, and yoga are being used to re-connect balance and stimulate health.

One way to successfully express and get your feelings out is to converse about them. This could be done out loud by speaking with a trustworthy friend, or on paper via a journaling practice.

Meditation is an additional treasured mind-body practice for becoming more present and balancing the mind. A consistent meditation practice is a predominantly effective way to assist the body moderate emotional responses and the associated neurochemical patterns that could otherwise flood the body with injurious stress hormones.

As soon as you could replace negative feelings with positive once, you will begin having encouraging results.

The beliefs you rely on about yourself and the world, your emotions, your memories, and your habits all could influence mental and physical health. These associations stuck between what is going on in your mind and heart, and what is taking place in your body, form the psycho-emotional origins of health and disease.

The body-mind connection occurs on both a physical and chemical level. The brain is the hardware that permits you to experience mental conditions that are considered the "mind." This idea of the "mind" covers mental states comprising thoughts, philosophies, attitudes, and emotions. Diverse mental states could positively or negatively touch biological running. This happens because the nervous, endocrine, and immune systems share a mutual chemical language, which permits constant communication between the mind and body via messengers such as hormones and neurotransmitters.

You might have witnessed this aspect of the body-mind association whenever you feel nervousness in your stomach when you feel anxious, or when you heart senses like it is coming out of your chest when you are under powerful stress.

These impact the preservation of health or the development of disease. For instance, emotions like anxiety could activate amplified stress hormones, which might subdue the immune system and set the phase for the development of infections or cancer.

Thoughts and emotions also convey vibrations that influence your biochemical, cellular, and complete physiological state. At a physical level, the body is compose of atoms and water, which are in a perpetual state of motion. The kind of movement or frequency at which atoms in a cell vibrate produces a form of wave energy that influences their structure and function. Science institutes that thoughts, words, and feelings could alter the crystal structure of water and cells, which could modify their function. Positive, kind, and stimulating thoughts and emotions vibrate in harmony with your cells because they share a similar frequency that allows them to function optimally.

THE BODY FEELS EMOTION!

Emotions such as fury, anxiety, guilt, anxiety, despondency, resentment, jealousy, depression, and stress could show within the body and add to imbalance and disease. When you experience emotional states such as sorrow, happiness, or anger, physiological sensations happen in different areas of your body. To stop the buildup of toxic emotions, you have to remain present and conscious. Paying attention makes you to pinpoint emotions as they arise, process them, and select how you react.

What you believe could lead to disease; the way you think and feel and the deep-seated belief arrangements you hold could all contribute to the growth of the disease. For case in point, feelings of anger or insecurity can upset the regular beating of the heart and the calm drift of the breath. Emotional and social support absolutely influences body-mind health. Persons with a lack of social support are more possible to have cardiovascular and other health difficulties than those with reliable and helpful relationships.

COMPREHENDING THE PSYCHO-EMOTIONAL ROOTS OF DISEASE

The beliefs you hold about yourself and the globe, your feelings, your memories, and your habits all stimulate mental and physical health. Let's go subterranean into the psycho-emotional roots of sickness. For centuries, healers have considered the connection between mental and physical health. In current years, science has begun to identify the prevailing connections through which emotional, divine, and behavioral factors can normally have emotional impact on the health outcomes.

A study in the arena of mind-body medicine is discovering, emotions and thought patterns could give to imbalances in the body, and therapies such as hypnosis, visual imagery, contemplation, yoga, and biofeedback are being used to reproduce balance and stimulate health. The opinions you have about yourself and the biosphere, your feelings, your memories, and your conducts all could influence mental and physical health. These links amid what is going on in your mind and heart, and what is going in your body, produce the psycho-emotional roots of health and disease. Let's take a closer observation.

The mind-body connection occurs on both a physical and chemical level. The brain is the hardware that makes you to experience mental states that are considered the "mind." This impression of the "mind" covers mental states comprising judgments, beliefs, attitudes, and feelings. Different mental states could positively or negatively upset biological working. This ensues since the nervous, endocrine, and immune systems have a collective chemical language, which permits constant communication between the mind and body through messengers such as hormones and neurotransmitters.

For illustration, neurological pathways link parts of the brain that process emotions with the spinal cord, muscles, cardiovascular system, and digestive region. This makes foremost life events, stressors, or emotions to produce physical symptoms. You might have experienced this part of the mind-body connection when you feel excitements in your stomach when you feel edgy, or when you heart senses like it is pounding out of your chest whenever you are beneath intense stress.

These interconnecting arrangements help to craft the mind-body connection that stimulates the conservation of health or the development of disease. For illustration, emotions like anxiety could activate increased stress hormones, which might subdue the immune system and set the stage for the development of infections or cancer.

THE INFLUENCE OF VIBRATION

Thoughts and emotions also convey vibrations that impact your biochemical, cellular, and complete physiological state. At a physical level, the body is made up of atoms and water, which are in a continuous state of motion. The type of movement or frequency at which atoms in a cell vibrate generates a form of wave energy that stimulates their structure and function.Science begins that judgements, words, and mental state could change the crystal structure of water and cells, which could change their function. Positive, kind, and exciting thoughts and emotions vibrate in unison with your cells because they have a related frequency that lets them to function normally. In fact, one study has found that the sort of vibrations or energy patterns that are conveyed by certain words and purposes are able to cause physical changes in DNA structure, which affect how the genetic code is interpreted to make different proteins that turn into the building blocks of your body. This might clarify why techniques such as affirmations and hypnotherapy could have such strong effects on the human body. Habitually, your thoughts are also communicated as words, which carry these robust vibrations and are then put into action as repetitive habits and behaviors that further impact health.

THE BODY FEELS EMOTION

Emotions such as rage, fear, guilt, nervousness, sorrow, dislike, jealousy, depression, and stress could be apparent in the body and add to imbalance and disease. For instance, you are somehow already acquainted with the way that fear could add to digestive upset or how tension can lead to headaches.

Whenever you experience emotional states such as sadness, happiness, or resentment, physiological sensations happen in different regions of your body. Scientists have fashioned maps of emotions, showing regions of the body that are actuated when study contributors experienced different emotions.

This connection is multidirectional. Emotional experiences affect the way you conduct yourself and the physiology in your body. In the other direction, your insight of these emotion-triggered bodily changes also impacts your consciously felt emotions Stuck or suppressed emotions seem to be particularly injurious to physical health.

One study showed that folks who suppress their emotions are more likely to have disturbances in the normal balance of the stress hormone cortisol equated to folks who easily express emotion. Over time, chronic psychological stress could change the way the body functions at a hormonal and immunologic level, contributing to the development and advancement of cancer and cardiovascular disease. For instance, studies indicate that having imbalances in the way that the nervous system controls the overall stress response, like producing too high or too low levels of stress hormones such as cortisol and epinephrine/adrenaline, might forecast early death in patients with metastatic breast cancer.

WHAT YOU HAVE FAITH IN CAN LEAD TO DISEASE

Because of this mind-body connection, the manner you think and sense and the deep-seated belief patterns you hold could all add to the development of disease. If you do not discover and deal with excruciating emotions, they could create an fundamental sense of anxiety, depression, or anger that can actually disrupt the body's natural capability to heal itself.

One collective way you might experience this collaboration of belief and physical sensations is when dealing with prolonged pain. Furthermore, pain is a combination of the physical sensations you experience, the emotions you feel, and the sense of the pain has for you. Emotional sorrow, physical pain, and other sensations share resemblances I n their neural pathways. For instance, feelings of anger or uncertainty could upset the regular beating of the heart and the peaceful flow of the breath.

These further triggers the sympathetic nervous system in the same way that happens when you are facing a menace, creating an even greater sense of unease and pain. You could see this type of physiology playing out in folks with a lack of social support, who are more probable to have cardiovascular and other health problems than those with consistent and supportive interactions. Another instance of the potent link between mind and body is that reducing symptoms of depression might enhance survival rates from cancer.

Psychological support is significant for dealing with emotions and changing beliefs and could help decrease depressive symptoms as well as inflammation. This proposes that emotional and social support absolutely impact mind-body health.

There is growing indication signifying that your mind and body are complicatedly connected, and wide acceptance that whatsoever is going on in your mind has some effects on your physical health. Brain imaging has shown meditation modifies your brain in helpful ways, and scientists have recognized thousands of genes that seem to be directly prejudiced by your subjective mental state. The mind-body connection is very real, and what you think does disturb your health.

In reality research proposes a tenacious negative state of mind is a danger factor for heart disease. Equally, contentment, hopefulness, life satisfaction and other optimistic psychological states are linked to a lower risk of heart disease. The investigating authors indicated that: "[The] research recommend that positive psychological well-being guards reliably against cardiovascular disease, self-sufficiently of old-style risk factors and ill-being. Precisely, optimism is most strongly allied with a lesser risk of cardiovascular events."

While some persons look to be born with a brighter disposition than others, meditation has been shown to enhance optimism and aid regulate mood. Meditative practices have also been shown to aid elevate your LDL cholesterol and lower your:

- Blood pressure
- Cortisol
- Heart rate

Such results are regular with a downregulation of your hypothalamic-pituitary-adrenal axis and sympathetic nervous system, both of which are over triggered by stress. Stress is also a celebrated risk factor for heart disease, making meditation all the more significant. In addition to encouraging heart health, meditation:

- Enhance emotional health and well-being
- Inspires self-awareness
- Aids fight addictions
- Improve sleep

- Strengthen feelings of compassion and kindness
- Increases attention span
- Diminishes anxiety and depression
- Manages pain
- Encourages concentration and memory
- Decreases stress
- Your Brain Benefits from Meditation

Meditation could be considered a type of "mental exercise" for your brain. The aim is to repeatedly draw your attention to your breath to the elimination of everything else. Every time your mind wanders, you try to softly bring it back to your breath.

According to Forbes.com, meditation assists us bond with and influence our minds:

"Through meditation, we get better acquainted with the behavior of our minds, and we advance our ability to normalize our experience of our environment, rather than letting our environment tell us how we experience life. With fresh neuroscientific discoveries, meditation as a practice has been revealed to accurately rewire brain circuits that increase both mind and body health. These advantages of meditation have appeared along with the revelation that the brain could be intensely transmuted through experience — a quality term 'neuroplasticity.'"

Certainly, neuroplasticity lets the nerve cells in your brain to regulate to new conditions and changes in their environs. The short-term effects of meditation consist of improving attention, hindering inflammation, lowering blood pressure and decreasing stress. Long-term meditation benefits, reaped over time with reliable practice, consist of heightened sympathy and gentleness, greater emotional flexibility and improved gray matter in brain areas connected to memory and emotional processing. As noted in one of the biggest studies to date on meditation and the human brain, different types of meditation produce diverse changes to your brain.

HOW TO TAP INTO YOUR OWN PSYCHIC ABILITIES

So far, we have talked about kinds of meditation and the real connection between our body and our meditation. Now we would be talking about psychic abilities. The psychic abilities can be said to be gifts that are embedded deep within our spirits. When the word psychic is used, often times we tend to imagine some fog machines or some manipulative Supernatural occurrences, most probably some smokes and mirrors and or some Supernatural unexplainable acts being performed.

Well you are not far from the truth but in other to actually make use of our extrasensory abilities we would have to firstly debunk this idea messed up in our head; the concept of the deception that we have about the word psychic. Psychic isn't black magic. Although there are con artists who uses the tactics of pretending to be a psychic in order to explore people. They come up with different schemes and has bastardized the word itself. Like psychic is all about magic. Being a psychic is being gifted. You decide how you make do with who you are and what you have.

WHO IS A PSYCHIC?

A psychic is a person that uses his natural abilities to go beyond the physical world. They feel, they hear, they sense, taste or basically live in their intuition beyond the boundaries of the natural world. Psychics tends to use their extrasensory perception to identity information that is not obvious to the normal senses.

This involves telepathy or clairvoyance. They can also perform acts that are inexplicable by natural laws. A broader way to define this is the ability to make use of sensory data on extremely deep emotional, physical or spiritual level. Really psychic would be phenomena that deal with the mind and soul.

A psychic basically lives in two worlds. Developing one's psychic abilities would require much practice, patience and value of one's self and abilities he own. Our instincts play a vital role psychologically. As a child, we tend to develop these skills, because as kids we make use of our senses more before we even get to understand basic things.

We see more, notice more and feel more. We tend to believe and receive anything life throws at us. As we grow, we begin to learn certain things to be unreal, things we had naturally received as kids we begin to see as being dumb. This is normal anyway which is what we call maturity. We are basically focused and fixed on one way; its either black or white. So, we tend to shut down our senses to anything that seems to be extra. We are no longer interested in cartoons that which made us laugh all day. We chose science as long as facts are obvious. We begin to believe that emotions and intuition are ant- science. We now believe our intuitions can be wrong while as a child you have once believed that it has to be right. In all this, all hope is definitely not lost. It's something you can absolutely deliberately decide to work on. It will require much work though, but a skill is a skill.

You can always shape it out to be productive to the degree at which you want it. Imagine being a parent and have left high school for years and your kid brings her homework for you to assist him with. There is every possibility that you must have forgotten how to go about such work. All you'd need to do is just to go over examples given and then it's easy to grab because you have gone through such class before. You'd have to go over your abilities till you become really familiar and master to it.

Another instance would be having a child with your divorced and have not had access to be with him for many years. It's going to take a lot for you to create that relationship again, the bonds between father and son. You'd have to start from trying to be friends just in a way to win his heart back to you. Same way one would need to re-establish a relationship between himself and his instincts.

You'd want to learn to trust your instincts to guide you. You'd need to look past the failures and get your instincts working, your intuition and perception. You'd have to give it a daily practice. You ought to deliberately want to know about stuff, how to read your environment and also relate with it. You'd just need to explore. You can also study people, use your senses right. Whilst at it, it is good to also pay attention to your most sensitive parts of your senses.

Keep practicing and be practical. Use every opportunity you get. These are things you can actually practice without anyone noticing anything. It's about you and you, so focus on you; you know, you are mastering, you are wielding your amazing psychic powers, the powers of your mind and soul. You ought to create a sound relationship with your sub consciousness such that there are things you just do and its by reflex. So, in building your psychic abilities consciously, it dawns into your sub consciousness. You can make do with your dreams and thoughts.

You can always pen down your dreams, however meaningful or un-meaningful it plays out. These are conscious ways to establish your sub consciousness. It's almost like hearing your phone vibrates before it rings. I am so use to my phone ringing that I tend to know when it's ringing even when I'm far away to even hear it ring. So, intuition happens in our daily life. One way or the other we all have these abilities. The only difference is how conscious we are to it.

ALL SAID, WE'D BE EXPLORING DIFFERENT TIPS TO IMPROVING OUR PSYCHIC ABILITIES.

I. HAVING QUIET TIMES

Meditation is quite needed in every field of our daily life. Someone ones said the mind grows into maturity to the degree it meditates on information and events it has been exposed to. When we have quiet time, we give room for our minds to journey through information and create thoughts and pictures, visions that can either be useful or useful. Useful in the sense of making do with it in your natural endeavours and useful by helping you to stretch your reasoning.

What you think about goes a long way. Meditation helps your minds to be sharp. It's easy to access information and even go back to things learnt. It can also help you travel beyond your normal state. When you think right, your mind is sharpened to be quick and sound. Having a quiet time helps you quiet down your mind, helps you to reduce tension, it changes your brain wave pattern. This helps you to be much sensitive to the natural world. Stuffs like yoga. When you are much calm in your mind, your senses are heightened and so it's sensitive to its surrounding. It also helps you to connect with the spiritual side of life.

2. BELIEVE IN GUTS

Most people have gotten to that point where they have totally shut out instincts because of past experiences. Some for the fear of being wrong has completely neglect their intuition. To them its all negative. Some others like I mentioned earlier has become a stickler for natural life event and see stuff like instincts as unreal. For the course they have silenced the flow.

Following your instinct may not always lead you in the totally right directions but it definitely comes true. You need to trust your guts. You need to learn to trust your guts. The question is "what if I'm wrong"? But then what if you are right? Why not trust your instincts. You can't because of a false experience shut something as precious as your inner spirit. It can guide you. Sometimes what you tend to look for around you could just be inside of you.

So, you'd need to let go of past failures, build your perception strong enough to follow your instincts. Trust your guts. Take that risk. Negative thoughts hinder psychic abilities. So, you can't afford to stay negative. You will need to have faith, create a positive environment around you. Think positively. Inspire yourself with another people's story that turned out right. Learn from them. Do not give room for doubts, and in no time, you would be master in using your gifts well.

3. TRY TO BE AT PEACE WITH EVERYONE

This helps you to stay sane around people. You won't have a reason to be uptight around anyone. Not everyone would love your psychic powers of course, they see you as creepy. But as much as possible, you can always avoid being creepy, try to make people understand mostly those that are close to you. Be quick to resolve a conflict, argue less. As a psychic you should avoid anything that will bring stress to your mind.

4- CREATIVITY

The ability of being a psychic that drags you into meditation would help you to work on your creativity; your Inner thoughts. Whatever you are exposed to plays out in your imagination and you can channel this into creating answers to situations, even situations that are yet to occur.

Such that when such situation occurs you are sensitive enough to provide answers and solution. You are able to think fast and act fact. You have become a blessing to the world around you.

Creative minds are thoughtful minds. You can build a castle in your heart. Weirdly as un-real as that could be, the more you think upon it the more exposed you are to go about it.

5-COMMUNICATE WITH YOUR SOUL

Your soul is a part of you that you can't do without. Oftentimes people do not know how to pay attention to that inner most part of them, the spirit. It's always speaking, and we should always try to pay attention to it. Sometimes you can actually speak to yourself and you find answers. This is because your soul communicates back to you.

No man knows himself better than his spirit; you can only grow up to learn to bring your mind to understand that which your spirit already knows. So, on the quest of uncovering your psychic abilities, pay attention to your soul and your spirit communing with you.

Sometimes this can also be a form of meditation. Sometimes, it can be so real like you can actually hear yourself audibly without speaking. It all depends on how deep you get into. In this you tend to know and fully understand yourself better.

6- EXPAND YOUR IMAGINATION (MIND TRAVEL)

Mind travel is such that you can be anywhere you want to. It's your creation. You can actually be in places you have never been to physically, but all in your mind. It doesn't have to be travelling around the world like an aspiration. It can actually be places you are planning to be in a couple of minute's even hours. Like the saloon, market, movies etc. You can actually let such activity play out in your mind. There a chance that what you had played out in your mind would eventually surface itself in reality. You would now begin to see each event as something that has happened before, like you went back in time kind of thing; time travel kinda thing. I know that thought, like this only happens in the movies, right? No, it just can happen to you if you practice.

7. BE POSITIVE MINDED ALWAYS

Do whatever you need to in order to feel content with your life. This might mean taking time out for yourself every once in a while or finding a hobby that you enjoy. It all boils down to what keeps a smile on your face. Stress and negativity get in the way of complete relaxation, which will help turn your focus to the supernatural. You must feel free spiritually before you can improve your psychic abilities; you have to let go of your worries before moving into a deeper state of consciousness.

8. DO NOT MISUSE YOUR PSYCHIC ABILITIES FOR PERSONAL GAIN

Your God-given gifts are always meant to help people. You have to make the choice to use them for good. People who become selfish with their special skills tend to lose them. For example, if you bet money after psychically predicting who will win boxing matches, prepare to forfeit your spiritual talents. Power like this is not given to anyone for winning money or anything of the sort. Always consider whether or not you're using your abilities for the collective good.

9. MAINTAIN A POSITIVE ATTITUDE AT ALL TIMES

One would need to have a sane and stable mind in other to delve into carrying out psychic activities, so you need to always maintain a positive mindset, a positive attitude. Always give yourself to things that make you happy. When you are happy and stress free, it is easy to access the spirituals and put your psychic abilities to use.

10. IMPROVE PSYCHOMETRIC SKILLS

There are artefacts and history objects. Spending time with these things gives you insights about history and you can actually create visions from each story from the items. You don't have to put pressure on yourself. Relax and try to actually feel the item and create pictures of what you actually see in your mind eyes. It broadens as you pay attention to the pictures you see. The more you see the realer it feels to you. You can eventually feel the actual emotions that the story has.

11. YOUR PHYSICAL HEALTH.

Your physical health is concerned with how you'd handle the spiritual. You need to be physical okay. It can actually affect your mental state which can now affect your access to the spirituals. You need to work on your wellbeing, stay healthy. Take of yourself. You can't be in pain and want to be active. It's bad energy to not be healthy. What about instances when you actually want to feel a particular object and you are actually hurt with your hands? One needs to try to stay in health as possible as he can.

12. OVERCOME YOUR FEARS

As a psychic you'd definitely be having a whole lot of encounters, some that are even hard to explain, some that will make your heartbeat skip, but you can't afford to be afraid. Fear can stop you from actualizing your dreams. Fear can put you in some kind of a bondage where you can't just let you out. Fear can actually keep you from touching the spiritual part of you. You can't give into fear. Fear of the unknown, fear of going to deep, fear of what you are going to find out. You shouldn't be in this theme over there and over here.

13. KEEP PRACTICING

You may not always see the need to go, but you have to keep going, keep practicing. You won't always have people encouraging you, you ought to keep encouraging yourself and keep pushing. Follow the progress of every step that has been given so far. Keep pushing yourself. If you didn't get it right, you can always go back again. Never give in to discouragements, no matter the situation. You keep pushing, keep striving for the top.

The psychic abilities are gifts to us. As we get older, we must see this as such that places the world's responsibilities on us. We can be of help to people around us. Being a psychic is neither odd nor weird. You don't have to feel that way. Rather you should see yourself as one that is gifted. You know, everyone can be a psychic.

This is not just meant for some people. We all have the ability to do these things. Its like our birth right. It's inborn. All we need to do is develop it and these points above you can work on yourself. Build confidence on your guts, meditation, deliberate practices with patience, in no time you'd be a psychic.

PSYCHIC POWERS AND ABILITIES

Throughout history they are different kinds of psychic powers and abilities. There are many with the supernatural powers that go beyond this natural realm. Many have channelled this into doing something positive. So being psychic is not about black magic and all. We get to know about these things because some have chosen to use their powers right and help others to see their past and can even predict the future. This is not about giving words from a bulk of cards together and controlling people. This is about being gifted and using it to serve a good purpose.

I am going to talk about a few psychic abilities as follows:

1. Clairvoyance

This has to do with seeing clearly. This is done with the mind eyes, where you actually see things and objects as though they were present, but they are not. There are clairvoyants that sees things like spirits as though they were humans and others that sees it like it's a picture before their eyes. Some people actually trained their minds this way to actually see this way, through imaginations and broad meditation. Others do by spiritual helps.

2. Clairaudience

Just like clairvoyance has to do with seeing, clairaudience has to do with audio, hearing things. You are able to hear thoughts or spirits as though they were humans standing in front of you. Sometimes, clairaudience can actually be hearing inanimate objects speak as though someone is speaking to your ears. Some other people call it audible thoughts.

3. Clairsentience

This has to do with sensing. When you can actually feel the presence of a spirit as if someone touched you. Some other times you can actually meet someone for the very first time and you actually have information concerning that person. This is one hell of a psychic ability! You can actually feel a person's pain without him saying anything to you. It's almost like your physical contact with that person sends information to your mind.

4. Clairalience

This has to do with smell. This ability helps you get information from just a smell. There is this instance where you can actually be in your room and you can actually perceive the smell of a late cousin or a late friend which indicates their presence in your room. This will usually happen if you have a connection with that person of course.

5. Clairgustance

This can really be weird, mostly if it's happening for the first time. You actually get to taste something that can be related to the deceased spirit you are channeling. Let's say for instance the person was a drug addict or he died of strong drugs, you'd get to taste drug without you being a drug user.

6. Claircognizance

This has to do with a clear knowing. You just tend to perceive that something is without prior information to prove it. You just know this is what it is and you are convinced about it. Its more like your spirit sends you information and you just bear witness with this without being informed by anyone. It comes with a strong feeling that you can't denied it authenticity and you can't prove it either, but you just know.

7. Aura Readings

An aura is described as an electromagnetic field that surrounds a person's body and its associated with their energy. This can actually be felt by everyone but can only be seen by some specific people.

Aura is such that can catch the vibes of the environment of the person. Aura can produce unique colors and vibration of different people but only some specific persons can actually be seen and can actually interpret the auras

8. Astral Projection

Astral projection is known as out of the body experience. This is done by which the soul of a person leaves the body of that person to travel around the universe. As strange as this may sound it is actually real.

This is usually not the total death of the person. It would almost look like the person just passed out but in a very short while the soul or consciousness of such a person must have travelled around the universe.

It is said that astral projection can happen under the influence of hypnosis and scientist considers this to be pseudoscience since the soul has not been proven to be in existence.

9. Automatic Writing

This is a subconscious writing. It is said that the psychic gets to write a whole document without knowing what he's doing as the words streams from his subconscious state of mind. It is said to be supernatural or spiritual. It will seem as though the psychic was possed.

10. Channeling

This is known as a medium in which a psychic is able to communicate with the deceased. It is usually a body. The body gets possessed by the spirit of a deceased. This was usually done maybe when there are specific information that is only known by the deceased or maybe to reach out to someone you had a strong relationship with in other to just be able to maybe see them again or speak to them, just to share company with them.

11. Divination

This would usually involve rituals, chants, incantations to a supernatural entity in other to ask questions or gain insights into a particular situation

12. PsychicHealing

This can often times be abused. Such that people can actually refuse going to see their physician. Energy healing is either done directly or from a distant.Its supposed to be an alternative not the main deal. Its an alternative medicine that has the ability to help the body heal.

Energy healing is not anti medicine or anti physicians. Its actually used to help out in some unavoidable situations.

13. Prescience

Prescience is when you have insight about a future event. It can either be through a dream or a vision or just a knowing, it can surface in your unplanned thoughts and then it just happens, not because you deliberately put it to play but because its just bound to happen. Its usually hard to be in control of it. It most times plays out like nature has to take his course. Psychic with such ability can most times feel helpless when they cant really be in control of it.

14. Psychic Surgery

Just like Psychic healing we have the psyhicsurgery. This is said to be a major practice by the philliphines and Brazilians in the mid 2oths. Its usually done when all hope is lost for the patient's recovery. The patients are healed of major health issues that would require a surgeon. Psychic surgery is done by a psychic surgeon. The psychic surgeon calls on spiritual guides to help heal the patient. The patient eventually gets restored to a normal state like they were never ill to begin with.

15. Psychometry

Ever had a situation where you have a contact with an object and you get deep insights on that object? You just have this connection with that object such that you see things that surrounds the object, maybe an event that happened with the object or a picture of the owner of it. Let's say you had your hands on a cloth that was used by someone who had a tragic ending in her life wearing the cloth and in having to touch the cloth you actually see the event play out like a vision in your mind. Psychics with this power can deliberately make do with this deliberately. Maybe to get facts about a particular event, they'd request for an object that relates with the event.

16. Remote Viewing

Remote viewing is such that a psychic gets to know information about a happening or an events or places and persons without being there. This is done without any physical senses.

Remote viewing can actually be learnt and practiced. You can actually just get to know also facts about people that it becomes hard to be lied to.

17. Retrocognition

Retro cognition is the ability to have information about the past that you were not present. Such past that it wasn't possible for you to learn by any means. It happens by either a dreams or a wake-up vision.

18. Scrying

In scrying, the psychic takes a look into a medium or an object to gather information. Like peeping or seeing through a mirror or cards or crytals, even stones. Fortune tellers are very well known for this.

19. Telekinesis

Telekinesis is from the word telekinetic. It is when a psychic channel a telekinetic power to carry out an activity. In this case he can move objects without touching them.

Hold that thought! This doesn't only happen in movies.

There psychics with this power. They can get a job done without breaking a sweat. They move things on their minds and see it physically moving.

20. Telepathy

Telepathy is the psychic ability to actually read people's mind, their thoughts. You can actually know what is going on in a persons head. Telepathy is such that you can actually make a person think about what you want them to think or even see what you want them to see. Telepathy can be a means of communing with someone without uttering a word. This can be done even when the other party is not a psychic.

There are so many psychic powers and I'm sure you can relate with this. Like I said earlier, if you have these powers, you are not alone, never see yourself as being weird or the odd one out. See yourself as one that is gifted and can certainly use this power to save your world. So never abuse your gifts, make do with it, channel it into something productive, something north living or during for.

I hope this guide helps you sharpen your abilities. This guide can only come in handy, so make do with it as we head on to the next chapter.

CHAPTER 7: TRUST YOUR INTUITION, IT NEVER LIES

Ever noticed times that you needed guidance and you felt you needed to either talk to someone or "follow your heart"? More often than not, you eventually heed to guidance from someone you believe would give the right direction. Some go as far as involving an expert. However, in some cases, it may not be wise to take such advice hook, line and sinker, which is why intuition cannot be neglected. Your intuition may not be as clear as that advice may be but because it is an intuition, it is existing. According to a clinical psychologist Sarah Schewitz states, "Intuition is that sneaking suspicion that you feel when something is not right, but you can't put your finger on why."

That hunch. Yes, that one right there. That is your intuition. While some are born with strong intuition, some are not. Either way, we all have an urge or inkling in our sense, which we tend to nurture overtime. Nonetheless, a person does not wake up to be confident of his or her intuition. It takes self-trust and self-love to become more in touch with it. Intuition is the ability to acquire knowledge without recourse to conscious reasoning. Different writers give the word "intuition" a great variety of different meanings, ranging from direct access to unconscious knowledge, unconscious cognition, inner sensing, inner insight to unconscious pattern-recognition and the ability to understand something instinctively, without the need for conscious reasoning. If you are a fan of Toy Story, then, you should know Buzz Lightyear. Buzz always presses his button to have his inner voice speak to him and whenever he hears it speak, he does whatever is said. That inner voice is intuition. You may choose to adhere to it or not. Although, it is advisable to.

Before you know how to use your intuition, you must be able to recognise it. Afterall, you cannot use what you don't have and now that you know that you have intuition, it is wise to get a full grasp of what it really is. Your intuition is a powerful force that you must use to your advantage. Learn how to open both your heart and mind to what you are capable of. Only then will your intuition be your guiding light on your journey through life. First, you get a calm or a hot feeling in your stomach. This is where the mental works with the physical. The urge or sense you get may affect your body system such that you either get a peaceful feeling or a tensed feeling in your stomach. "Many people describe their intuition as a feeling in her chest or in their stomach. Often, it comes as a tightness in those areas and the feeling that something is off," says Schewitz. Also, when you don't listen to your intuition, you may actually cause more stress in your life. Physical signs like having anxiety or being sick may slowly creep into your life because your intuition is trying to tell you that you need a change. "Physical signs in the early stages might feel like something's not quite right or something feels off.

As many of us tend to ignore our intuition, the feeling will naturally grow to something more severe like anxiety, even depression can be a physical sign that you are not living life the way you know you want to be. If these more obvious feelings are ignored, ultimately our body can manifest illness as an extreme way of letting us know we need to make some kind of change in our life," Holmes. Sometimes, it's a tightness in your chest or throughout your body. Brain fog. Pressure in your forehead or waking up with a palpitating heart. A sense of unease in your stomach. This may be a signal that you need to make a change. When you feel anxious, it's your body's way of telling you something's off. These physical symptoms also reveal whether or not the decision taken is the right one. Your intuition is everything, it affects your reasoning, your emotions and your body system.

Furthermore, confidence sets in as you believe your mind (your intuition) has provided the 'best' decision even if it does not seem rational. Those conversations you keep having with your inner mind help to give clarity and breeds confidence towards accepting what your mind says. Sometimes, it would not make sense but because you believe in your intuition, you tend to be more relaxed and take the decision without considering the consequences it may attract. You would agree with me that when you listen to your intuition, you normally feel happy, but if you choose to ignore it, a wave of uneasiness may come over you.

For instance, you may choose to listen to your ego to make a safe but wrong decision instead of listening to what your heart is trying to tell you. "Your intuition is trying to tell you something when you feel uneasy. This uneasiness can show up as an unfocused mind, pressure in the body like the chest, or an uneasy gut reaction," says Khorshid. In cases where you feel a sense of emptiness or sadness in your heart. It's important to notice this and be curious to investigate the disharmony. What makes you feel sad or lonely? Is your head (what you think will make you happy, or your expectations and desires) misaligned with your heart? You also have a sense of confidence when you note down times that you have trusted your guts and when your guts turned out to be valid and accurate.

The next indicator happens to be my favourite one: your intuition re-occurs. You may notice the same opportunities keep knocking on your door. You may keep having the same lucid dreams. But the point is your intuition keeps coming, especially when you have not been heeding to it. When your intuition tries to communicate with you, it may try to get your attention by forcing you to notice little patterns throughout your life. Been wanting to get out of that relationship or get a new job? Your intuition may subtly let you notice certain hints to help you take that brave step. There's a reason why that particular thought keeps on popping up in your head. It's your intuition trying to speak to you. Be more receptive to these subtle nuances so you can allow your life to flow much easier. "The best way to determine if it is your intuition telling you something is that you will have the sense that it 'won't go away.' In other words, that sensation of knowing you should or should not do something simply keeps dogging you," says Anita Marchesani. Your intuition may re-occur in diverse ways, depending on which one you pay most attention to. It could keep hitting you with physical symptoms or draw your attention to things you probably would not pay attention to.

This moves me to the next hint, which is my second favourite. Your intuition comes with ease and when at ease. Have you ever had those "I said it!" moments when you were in the shower or driving your car? That's an example of your intuition trying to talk to you. When you allow your mind to rest (i.e. meditation), your mind opens up and allows your thoughts and emotions to flow through. "Your intuition talks to you when you are less busy, when you sleep, when are you not trying to push for it, when you take your mind off what you are seeking," says MacFadyen.

Also, you may notice your thoughts are being pulled in a certain direction. Your intuition is usually always there to guide you in the right direction, but sometimes you miss the signs or choose to ignore them. However, if you continue to notice that your brain wanders back to a particular thought, then you might want to slow down and investigate why you're feeling this way. Very important to note is that your instinct and intuition will not in sync. Sometimes your rational instinct (AKA your ego) will try to protect you from failure or making a mistake. While your instinct is there to help you survive, your intuition will sometimes try to fight against your fears of failure so you can make the right decision and go after your dreams. Instinct is often misinterpreted as intuition and its reliability considered to be dependent on past knowledge and occurrences in a specific area. For example, someone who has had more experiences with children will tend to have a better instinct about what they should do in certain situations with them. This is not to say that one with a great amount of experience is always going to have an accurate intuition.

According to the works of Daniel Kahneman, intuition is the ability to automatically generate solutions without long logical arguments or evidence. Our intuition is based upon our core beliefs. Those values by which we live and breathe by. They are formed by our environment and families as we grow but circumstances throw a wrench into our daily plans. When it comes time to make the tough decisions you must allow your intuition to have a say. Get in touch with your emotions and embrace your inner self. That inner self will help you as intuition comes from the right hemisphere of the brain which controls the non-verbal and expressive part.

Intuition, as a gut feeling based on experience, has been found to be useful for business leaders for making judgement about people, culture and strategy. Intuition is challenging to define; despite the huge role it plays in our everyday lives. Steve Jobs called it, for instance, "more powerful than intellect." But however, we put it into words, we all, well, intuitively know just what it is. Pretty much everyone has experienced a gut feeling -- that unconscious reasoning that propels us to do something without telling us why or how. Whenever we are at crossroad, facing that dilemma, wondering what to do and trying to get the right direction, our inner voice is always there to steer us right.

Now that you know what intuition is able and you can recognise it, you need to know how to use the weapon you have got.

First, listen to that inner voice. "It's very easy to dismiss intuition," says Burnham. "But it's a great gift that needs to be noticed. "Rather than ignore the guidance of intuitions and gut feelings, you need to listen to it. "Everybody is connected to their intuition, but some people don't pay attention to it as intuition," Burnham say. "I have yet to meet a successful businessman that didn't say, 'I don't know why I did that, it was just a hunch. '"In order to make our best decisions, we need a balance of intuition -- which serves to bridge the gap between instinct and reasoning -- and rational thinking, according to Francis Cholle, author of The Intuitive Compass. But the cultural bias against following one's instinct or intuition often leads to disregarding our hunches -- to our own detriment. Just like a journey begins with a step, following an intuition begins by listening to that intuition. The more you listen to your intuition, the more confident you become of it.

Also, you need to take time for solitude. If you want to get in touch with your intuition, a little time alone may be the most effective way. As aforementioned, your intuition comes with ease and when at ease. Just as solitude can help give rise to creative thinking, it can also help us connect to our deepest inner wisdom. When you are alone and your mind is at rest, it will be easy for 'your inner voice to speak'. Intuitive people are often introverted, according to Burnham. But whether you're an introvert or not, taking time for solitude can help you engage in deeper thought and reconnect with yourself.

"You have to be able to have a little bit of solitude; a little bit of silence," she says. "In the middle of craziness ... you can't recognize [intuition] above all of the noise of everyday life." You don't expect to get a clear direction when there are distractions around that can affect the mental intrapersonal communication. There are external factors that can influence the message your inner voice intends to deliver but there could also be internal factors such as prejudice and doubts, that could affect the communication. Therefore, it is often not enough to be in a quiet place, a person must also have a 'peaceful mind' to be able to listen to his or her intuition. Moving on, you become creative. "Creativity does its best work when it functions intuitively," writes researcher and author Carla Woolf. In fact, creative people are highly intuitive, explains Burnham, and just as you can increase your creativity through practice, you can boost your intuition. In fact, practicing one may build up the other. Creativity and intuition work hand in hand such as improving on one would in turn boost the other. The more you listen to your intuition, the more creative you become and the more you tend to create, the more you need to listen to your intuition. What happens when you hang onto things you don't need? You put a cover over understanding, clarity and compassion. You see things not as they are but as you want to see them. This stifles creativity which is where intuition lives. Follow your intuition to its logical conclusion and you will see positive results.

Also, you need to practice mindfulness. Meditation and other mindfulness practices can be an excellent way to tap into your intuition. As the Search Inside Yourself Leadership Institute explains, "Mindfulness can help you filter out mental chatter, weigh your options objectively, tune into your intuition and ultimately make a decision that you can stand behind completely. "Mindfulness can also connect you to your intuition by boosting self-knowledge. A 2013 study published in the journal Perspectives on Psychological Science showed that mindfulness -- defined as "paying attention to one's current experience in a non-judgmental way" -- may help us to better understand our own personalities. And as Arianna Huffington notes in Thrive, increased intuition, compassion, creativity and peace are all wonderful side effects of meditating. Meditation feeds the mind and heals the soul. When you are given to meditation, you will find yourself attracting positivity. Hence, your inner voice will provide the direction you genuinely need. If a thought comes to you, go with it, see where it takes you. Maybe it's leading you to a new contact, new job or opportunity that you've been looking for.

In addition, you need to be observant (of everything). Being intuitive would demand you to be like a hawk. You need to pay attention to your environment, the people in the environment and the occurrences. Your intuition often communicates through things in the environment. This is when you tend to notice coincidences and incidence. "The first thing to do is notice - keep a little journal, and notice when odd things happen,"

Burnham says. You'll gain a keen sense for how often coincidences, surprising connections and on-the-dot intuitions occur in your daily life - in other words, you'll start to tap into your intuition. In the same vein, pay attention to your body.

Intuitive people learn to tune into their bodies and heed their "gut feelings. "If you've ever started feeling sick to your stomach when you knew something was wrong but couldn't put your finger on what, you understand that intuitions can cause a physical sensation in the body. Our gut feelings are called gut feelings for a reason -- research suggests that emotion and intuition are very much rooted in the "second brain" in the gut. Earlier, we saw how the mental and the physical connection. Hence, you need to be able to tell what your mind is saying by paying attention to what your body is saying. The physical indicators help to know what the intuition is after all and what decision to take. Importantly, you need to connect deeply with others. Mind reading may seem like the stuff of fantasy and pseudo-science, but it's actually something we do every day. It's called empathic accuracy, a term in psychology that refers to the "seemingly magical ability to map someone's mental terrain from their words, emotions and body language," according to Psychology Today. "When you see a spider crawling up someone's leg, you feel a creepy sensation," Marcia Reynolds writes in Psychology Today. "Similarly, when you observe someone reach out to a friend and they are pushed away, your brain registers the sensation of rejection. When you watch your team win or a couple embrace on television, you feel their emotions as if you are there.

Social emotions like guilt, shame, pride, embarrassment, disgust and lust can all be experienced by watching others. "Tuning into your own emotions, and spending time both observing and listening to others face-to-face can help boost your powers of empathy, says Reynolds. You do well with the information you have gathered about things, occurrences and most importantly, people. This will aid your inner voice into providing a direction that pertains and suits the situation. What you think is mostly a product of what you are exposed to. Therefore, if you rub minds with people more often, you will be able to know how they think and how to relate with them. Of course, your intuition would also make it an easier task. Also, you need to be flexible and dynamic. You really need to stop doing the same old thing day after day. Many times, your intuition and dreams are telling you they need to have both space and activity. A stifled personality becomes bored easily and I know you don't want that!

Next, pay attention to those dreams!! Those lucid yet vivid dreams, you need to pay attention to them. Burnham recommends paying attention to your dreams as a way to get in touch with your mind's unconscious thinking processes. Both dreams and intuition spring from the unconscious, so you can begin to tap into this part of your mind by paying attention to your dreams. "At night, when you're dreaming, you're receiving information from the unconscious or intuitive part of your brain," says Burnham. "If you're attuned to your dreams, you can get a lot of information about how to live your life."

Sometimes, we tend to forget the dreams we have once we wake up or five minutes after we do. But, in a case whereby we remember, we might need to write it down as it could be a form of communication from your inner voice, especially when that dream keeps coming. It is wise to pay attention to it. Even the daydreams and fantasies can count as a form of communication. What happens when you do this is that your mind and your heart align and your brain provides a vivid description of it. Are you distracted? Do you seek things that don't help you? It's time to stop running away from life and get involved. The cognitive side is the rational part of the brain. What you need to do is pay attention to your dreams. They are fuelling your intuition, but you are ignoring that part of your brain function. Combining our dreams with our emotional side is a secret most people are not privy to.

They think it's easier to use one or the other but you're only getting half the picture. Often, you feel like something is about to happen and many times, these hunches come in dreams or a dream state but if you push off the emotional side and go logically, you're missing a big piece of the puzzle. Listen to your dreams. What are your dreams telling you? Is there a problem that is bothering you and you don't have the answer? Let your dreams work it out. Give the responsibility to your dreams and take the pressure and stress off of your own shoulders. Quickly, I will like to add that few things stifle intuition as easily as constant busyness, multitasking, connectivity to digital devices and stress and burnout. According to Huffington, we always have an intuitive sense about the people in our lives -- on a deep level, we know the good ones from the "flatterers and dissemblers" -- but we're not always awake enough to our intuition to acknowledge the difference to ourselves. The problem is that we're simply too busy. "We always get warnings from our heart and our intuition when they appear," she writes in Thrive. "But we are often too busy to notice."

Moving on, you need to deliberately let go of negative emotions. Strong emotions -- particularly negative ones -- can cloud our intuition. Many of us know that we feel out of sorts or "not ourselves" when we're upset, and it may be because we're disconnected from our intuition. "When you are very depressed, you may find your intuition fails," says Burnham. "When you're angry or in a heightened emotional state ... your intuition [can] fail you completely. "The evidence isn't just anecdotal: A 2013 study published in the journal Psychological Science showed that being in a positive mood boosted the ability to make intuitive judgments in a word game. That's not to say that intuitive people never get upset -- but your intuition will fare better if you're able to mindfully accept and let go of negative emotions for the most part, rather than suppressing or dwelling on them. In other to let the good 'stuff' in, you need to let the bad 'stuff' out.

Take a pen and note down times you are trusted your guts. This will not only guide you to applying a direction to a similar issue, but it will also boost your confidence. This will also build awareness of how you felt when you listened to your intuition. Trust is a big word that most people aren't willing to embrace. Are you ready to trust your intuition? Are you ready to get the kind of results you've been missing in your life?

It's time to start trusting your intuition to do more for your life than its doing now. The majority of people are living life on autopilot. The get up in the morning, go to work, come home, eat and then go to sleep. It's the same day-to-day life that stifles both creativity and intuition. You would be able to match your intuition with physical signals. As your instincts become honed with practice, you get better at pattern recognition. You start noticing the small signals in your emotions and what pulls you. This helps you notice your intuition sooner and make even better decisions.

You also need to take power from the inner critic. Intuition gets louder when you quiet the noise of the mind. When you notice your inner critic going in circles, it's an invitation to pay attention. You need to recognise the voices in your head and see how they either agree or conflict. Do these voices help the situation or not? Which voices are you allowing to take center stage? You don't need to try to resist the inner critic, because that'll only make it stronger. Instead, take away its power by developing your awareness of it. Acknowledge the insecurities it brings up. Recognize the voices that aren't serving you, so you can identify your most authentic inner voice. That's the voice of your heart, your soul. Allow it to have a conversation with your inner critic, then take center stage. According to Alan Alda, "At times you have to leave the city of your comfort and go into the wilderness of your intuition. What you'll discover will be wonderful. What you'll discover is yourself."

Following your intuition is a daily practice, because the inner critic likes to distract. But it gets easier to ignore as you build awareness of it. Stop caring what others think. As much as you get criticise by people, an inner voice could also serve as a critic, hence, you need to be able to distinguish between the inner critic and the right inner voice. The earlier you do this, the better. We may be the greatest obstacles to our dreams. So we must get out of our own way, guiding the mind and trusting our inner voice. I've come to realize there's no point pursuing what you're not truly passionate about, because you won't be able to throw your full heart into it. It will wither away. If we are able to get the negativity out of the way, we are sure to emerge victorious.

The pineal gland, corium or epiphysis cerebra is a small endocrine gland in the brain, present in most vertebrates. This gland, the pineal gland produces melatonin. Melatonin is a serotonin derived hormone which modulates sleep pattern in both circadian and seasonal cycles. The pineal gland derived its name from a pinecone form. This is because the shape of the gland resembles a pinecone. Perceived from the angle of biological evolution, the pineal gland represents an end of atrophied photoreceptor.

Simple eye often times called a pigment pit can be referred to a form of eye or an optical arrangement which comprises of a single lens without an elaborate retina such as occurs in most vertebrates. The simple eye has a distinction from the compound eye which is multi lens. The eyes of humans and other large animals are classified as simple. They can also be called camera eyes because they are single unlike some animals that have multi lens eyes. The eyes of humans are referred to as camera eyes because a single lens collects images and focuses on the retina or film.

In some animals like reptiles and amphibians, their epithalamiums is linked to a light sensing organ known as parietal eye which is also called pineal or the third eye. The parietal eye is a part of the epithalamus present in the species of fishes, amphibians and is also present in reptiles. This third eye is situated atop the head. It is photoreceptive in nature and is closely associated with the pineal gland.

The pineal gland is laden with the responsibility of rhythmicity and hormone production for thermoregulation. In humans, the pineal gland is perceived to be the principal seat of the soul. The pineal gland can also be considered as a neuroanatomical structure without special metaphysical qualities.

WHERE IS THE PINEAL GLAND LOCATED?

The pineal gland is located in the epithalamiums, which is near the center of the brain, between the two hemispheres, tucked in a groove where the two halves of the thalamus join. One of the neuroendocrine secretory circumventricular organs is the pineal gland. In these organs, there does not exist the blood brain barrier at the capillary level.

What it does:

The pineal gland is known for its production and regulation of some hormones, including melatonin. The Pineal Gland is situated in the centre of the brain, behind and above the pituitary gland. The Pineal Gland is the gland with the highest concentration of energy in the body. That's because it is bathed in highly charged cerebrospinal fluid (CSF) and has more blood flow per cubic volume than any other organ. The Pineal Gland is also the primary source of the body's melatonin.

PINEAL GLAND AND MELATONIN

The activation of melatonin by the pineal gland is spurred by darkness and light inhibits it. Our body needs melatonin for its effect on our moods, circadian rhythms, immunity system, and the quantity and quality of our sleep. Added to the host of things melatonin does in the body, it also has an anti-aging effect on the body.

Not only does melatonin reduces how the body ages, it also is an anti-stress agent and an antioxidant. After melatonin is released into the body, it travels through the CSF and enters nearby blood vessels. It does this in order to be adequately distributed throughout the body. Bad moods and mood swings can be caused by low level of melatonin production. Also, we can trace depression and seasonal disorders to the low level of melatonin production.

PINEAL GLAND-HOW IS SEROTONIN AND DMT PRODUCED

Other neurochemicals such as pinoline and DMT are produced as a result of a healthy and activated pineal gland. These neurochemicals coordinate emotional and physical processes on a cellular level. The DMT and the pinoline connect the mind and the body. Serotonin is a precursor of these two neurochemicals. We can say that the pineal gland plays a key role in expanding consciousness because the highest concentration of serotonin is found in the pineal gland. The brain begins to produce serotonin, a biochemical that expands consciousness when the pineal gland is activated. Taking into consideration that the highest concentration of serotonin is found in the Pineal Gland, we may say that the Pineal Gland plays a key role in expanding consciousness.

Ancient civilizations believed in their ancient traditions that activating the Pineal Glands equals to the opening of the Third Eye. Most vertebrate species including human's beings possess a pineal gland. An important exception that we cannot help but mention is the hagfish and the lamprey. Due to evolution, some more developed vertebrates have lost pineal glands. Melatonin plays a role in the regulation of sleep patterns as stated earlier. These sleep patterns are also called circadian rhythms.

Not only does the pineal gland regulates sleep patterns, it also is actively involved in the regulation of the female hormone levels. It may also affect fertility and the female menstrual cycle. This is as a result of the melatonin that is produced and excreted by the pineal gland. Melatonin which is secreted by the pineal gland also helps in protecting against cardiovascular issues such as atherosclerosis and hypertension.

Also on the pineal gland and melatonin, it can be recalled as earlier stated that melatonin which is produced by the pineal gland helps in the regulation of sleep patterns, it can also be noted that a sleep disorder could be a sign that the pineal gland is not secreting the correct amount of melatonin the body needs. It is believed that one can detox and activate their pineal gland to improve sleep and open your third eye. Though there are no scientific research to back up and support these claims.

The pineal gland also stabilizes mood. Study suggests that the size of ones pineal gland may indicate a risk of certain mood disorders. The lower pineal gland volume may increase ones risk of developing schizophrenia and some other mood disorders. Schizophrenia is a chronic psychiatric disorder. People who are diagnosed with this disorder experience distortions of reality. They often experience delusions and or hallucinations. Some people think that having schizophrenia creates a double or split personality which is commonly termed as dissociative identity disorder. These two disorders differ one from the order.

According to some researches, there is a connection between impaired pineal gland function and cancer risk. A study that was once carried out on rats showed that over exposure to light led to cellular damage and an increased risk for colon cancer. Just like other parts of the body, it is possible for the pineal gland to develop issues or malfunction. If something goes wrong in the pineal gland, it can lead to a hormone imbalance which in turn can affect many other systems in the human body. If the pineal gland becomes impaired, sleep patterns becomes distorted and disrupted. This can show up in lack of sleep also known as insomnia and jet lag.

Also, because melatonin which is produced by the pineal gland interacts with female hormones, any complications with the pineal gland may affect the menstrual cycle and fertility. According to the location of the pineal gland, it is situated close to many other important structures and it interacts heavily with fluids in the body and also the blood.

If one develops a pineal gland tumor it affects many other organs in the body causing a host of things. Some signs and symptoms of tumor include:

- Seizures
- Headache
- Disruption in memory
- Nausea
- Damage in vision and other senses

HOW TO AWAKEN YOUR PINEAL GLAND?

Adoption of vegan diet: one way to awaken your pineal gland is to go on a diet. Preferably a vegan diet should be adopted. One that contains lots of green vegetables and raw plants. If you engage in the consumption of foods that has additives, pesticides and additional sweeteners, you stand risk of toxifying your pineal gland. Some foods that stand as an obstacle in awakening your third eye are meat and dairy products. Foods that contain bovine and porcine antibiotics. Also, medications and growth hormones that are not compatible with your spiritual health and also your physical health.

Darkness: the darkness when utilized properly can serve as another way of awakening your third eye. Both the light and darkness can help your pineal gland activation. To mimic the night during the day, draw down your curtain, make sure your bedroom or living room, whichever you are using is as dark as possible during the dream time. A little light can interrupt the process. Be sure to turn off all appliances that can emit light.

Kundalini yoga: this method is another effective way of awakening your pineal gland due to some specific set of movements. Effective practice of this yoga will activate your pineal gland. Kundalini yoga helps you connect to the cosmic energy with the physical body and root it to earth. By doing this, you are activating the 33 spinal points until it reaches the third eye and the crown chakra.

Essential oils and natural remedies: aromatherapy is another way of activating your pineal gland. This is because the nose is more like a straight and direct pathway to the nose. Aromatherapy will be a good practice for those who want to rebirth their pineal gland. Different essential oils will help you stimulate this gland: sandalwood, myrrh, pine, pink lotus, clary sage. There are also other natural remedies that have the same effect on the pineal gland. The essential oils: coconut oil, turmeric, spiraling, need oil, walnuts, blue-green algae, lemon water, ginseng, sea moss, oregano oil

Fluoride and Mercury free: the consumption of excess synthetic fluoride results in the calcification of the pineal gland which in turn also disturbs the production of melatonin. A water filtration system that takes the fluoride out of tap water, toothpaste with natural fluoride are solution to reduce the fluoride absorption through the pores.

Also, the mercury from dental amalgam filling is highly toxic and is poisoning our Pineal gland whenever we drink hot tea, coffee, or a soup. We can go to a mercury free dentist to get rid of the amalgam fillings. Mercury is also found in a lot of vaccines in the form of methylmercury (Theresa) which binds to the brain and is very difficult to detox. A fresh juice made of cilantro will help you get rid of the mercury in your body.

Precious stones: When lying down, place a crystal over your third eye and watch the wonders it words on activating your third eye. There are lots of crystals you can use to achieve this such as Blue Jasper, Cestine, Fluorite, Sapphire and moon stone. Violet or indigo hues between the eyebrows when left there during meditation also works.

Lose the sunglasses: If you are a huge sunglasses fan, you may be hindering your third eye activation as the third eye, just like the normal eyes need sunlight. In order for us as humans to function properly, we need to expose our physical eyes to indirect sunlight. Because of the presence of a photoreceptor in the pineal gland, light reflected by the retina activates it. So next time you want to detox your pineal gland and activate your third eye, remember to keep in mind that the sunshades should be kept away.

Sunbathing and sun gazing: If we understand light and it's importance in our lives, we can properly utilize it and use it in awakening the third eye. Light, as we know is a basic nutrient of life. Plants as a well as humans needs light to survive. The way we use this light determines how it can help is in our evolution process. The hypothalamus, the pituitary and the pineal gland are all extremely sensitive and responsive to light. According to a research carried out in 2002, a new type of eye Light receptors were found. They were situated in the retina and the scientists were able to discover a third photoreceptor which contained a light-sensitive pigment called melanopsin. These cells send messages to the hypothalamus SCN (suprachiasmatic nucleus). The SCN is responsible for controlling circadian rhythms (sleep, alertness, hormones, digestive functions).

When we are focused and highly motivated, we can relax and be more aware of how we can access every level of our energy. Sun gazing is an ancient method or way of improving health as it induces us into a state as clairvoyance is heightened and the ability to subsist without water and go without food for many days. When the sun sets is a perfect time to practice sun gazing as well as when it rises. We should keep in mind that the human eyes are very sensitive and overexposure of light during the day can harm the eyes.

So go ahead and feed your eyes with solar light, at sunrise or sunset, especially when you seek to decalcify your pineal gland. Make it a habit of practicing sun gazing for at most a minute daily.

TO GET THE BEST FROM SUN GAZING, FOLLOW THESE RULES

Engage in sun gazing within the hour after sunrise or before sunset. Doing it this way helps prevents eye damage. To get the maximum benefit from sun gazing, it's best to feed your eyes on the sun barefoot, in contact with the Earth: sand, mud. One very important process in activating the pineal glans is walking on your barefoot. Research carried out by researchers shows that each toe has a link to a specific gland. Walking directly on the earth serves as a great way of stimulating your glands. For instance, the big toe is linked to the pineal gland. Also, the second toe has a link with the pituitary gland while the third toe is linked with the hypothalamus. The fourth toe is linked to the thalamus and the fifth toe which can also be called the pinky toe is linked to the amygdala. When we wear shoes, the soles serve as an insulator from electricity. These soles prevent us from interacting directly with the energetic field that is present in the earth. When you walk barefoot you create a magnetic field in and around your body, now combine walking barefoot with sun gazing.

You experience more energy as your body is in tune with the earth's energetic field the magnetic field that is created when we walk barefoot and gaze at the sun smoothens our vibrational frequency. It also is in sync with the earth's vibrational frequency. This can be likened to how a battery is charged as our physical body is also charged by engaging in these activities. Lastly, starting with a 10 seconds session. Increase the time by 10 seconds each day. Do not overexpose your eye to the sun as this can damage the eyes.

THE PINEAL GLAND AND THE ENDOCRINE SYSTEM

One fundamental way of expanding consciousness and restoring the health and vibration frequency of the body is to balance and activate the pineal gland. The endocrine system we possess is an important link activator between the physical function and the spiritual experience. The endocrine system includes the following glands: the pituitary, the pineal, hypothalamus, thyroid, parathyroid, adrenals, pancreas, and ovaries/testes. Just like the nervous system, these glands do not use electrical impulses, to effect changes in our body, emotion, energy level or cognition. These glands use hormones to impact the up mentioned plans they activate on.

What are hormones? Simply put, hormones are chemical messengers that circulate through our bloodstream and coordinate important body functions. They increase or decrease the nerve impulses level. The Pineal Gland, the hypothalamus and the pituitary have significant roles to play in the activation and awakening process of our spiritual development. As we go further on how to awaken your third eye, we shall discuss the strong link.

THE HYPOTHALAMUS – PITUITARY LINK

The Hypothalamus plays an essential role in linking the nervous to the endocrine system, and in activating the Pineal Gland. The limbic system which is the center if our emotions and feelings is connected to the hypothalamus. Asides from our emotions and feelings, the hypothalamus with the pituitary gland affect most of the major systems and organ functions in the body. The hypothalamus and the pituitary gland regulate all of our basic survival needs and processes which are hunger, thirst, fatigue, sleep, growth, pain relief, blood pressure, body temperature. Neurohormones which are produced by the hypothalamus communicate with the pituitary gland.

This serves as a signalling of the release or inhibition of key pituitary hormones, which harmonize and activate the Pineal Gland function. By signalling and directing the pituitary, the hypothalamus plays a critical role in the endocrine system. It also has a big impact on the "awakening" of the Pineal Gland.

THE ROLE OF THE PITUITARY GLAND IN SPIRITUAL AWAKENING

Seven hormones are secreted by the anterior lobe of the pituitary gland. These hormones influence lactations, the release of testosterone, the production of the human growth hormone, thyroid and the sex hormones. Unlike the anterior lobe of the pituitary gland, the posterior lobe does not produce hormones. Rather it stores and releases two important hormones which are produced by the brain itself. These hormones are oxytocin and vasopressin. Oxytocin stimulates maternal instincts and sexual pleasure while Vasopressin influences circadian rhythms, the reabsorption of water into the bloodstream, and the paternal protective instincts.

The health of the pituitary gland is very important as it has a very strong impact on our growth. We should also note that the health of the pituitary gland is equally essential git the activation of the pineal gland. When the pineal gland and the pituitary gland begin to vibrate harmoniously or in synchronisation, we are more inspired, and we are renewed on both the spiritual and the physical plan.

PINEAL GLAND AND SPIRITUALITY

The activated Pineal Gland was part of the spirituality from ancient times. We can find it's pinecone depiction in art and artefacts and in many ancient traditions as well. Enlightenment and immortality stem out of a healthy pineal gland. It is safe to say that is the reason why the ancient Egyptians worshipped the pineal gland. They also kept the pineal gland separately during the mummification process. This pinecone shaped gland represents a perfect Fibonacci sequence. And as. we already know, a Fibonacci sequence is the symbol of growth. So, the Pineal Gland is a symbol of evolution and continuous progress through its shape also.

As many wisdom traditions believe, when performing at its ultimate capacity, the pineal gland produces important biochemical, such as <u>DMT (Dimethyltryptamine)</u> or the "spirit molecule" which is a prime catalyst for higher states of universal consciousness, intuition and enlightenment. Also, esoteric schools believe that having a blocked pineal gland has as result confusion and delusion, a tendency to over-analyze, depression and anxiety, paranoia, pessimism and all other kinds of low vibrational emotions and feelings.

When perceived from the spiritual point of view, the secretion of melatonin by the pineal gland d helps the body and the mind maintain a sense of quietness. This gives us more access to higher consciousness. The DMT and the pinoline produced by the Pineal Gland are both psychoactive. They change our perception, consciousness, cognition, behaviour and also our mood, as a result. Ancient Egyptians and Zoroastrians used pinoline as an opening gate to visions and dream states in the conscious mind. Pinoline resonates with the pulse of life, with the primordial vibration frequency, at about 8 cycles per second.

DMT is naturally produced by the body. It is produced in different types of experiences like the pleasure you get during sexual intercourse, a close or near-death experience, deep meditations and also extreme physical stress. DMT also when released into the blood stream alters our dream consciousness. This occurs during rapid eye movement phase of sleep. DMT can also be referred to as the Spirit Molecule. This is because of the close relationship between DMT and visionary experiences.

PINEAL GLAND, VIBRATIONS AND MAGNETISM

The human heart is said to be as powerful as the brain. In fact, it us a powerful brain. Rhythmicity or rhythmic vibrations has a strong effect on the physical body and the health in general. The rhythmic vibrations goes a long way in affecting our mood, emotions, cognition, etc. It has also been discovered that music influences our state of health through vibrations. It is safe to note that vibrations are transmitted from the human body. Just as vibrations are transmitted from the human body, they can also be interpreted by the body. This sync or resonance emerges when two wave forms begin to oscillate exactly at the same rate. When the hypothalamus and the pituitary entrain with the pulsing vibration of the pineal gland, the whole system is in harmony. The North Star, according to ancient tradition symbolizes the source of the original pulse. Some datists reason that the vibrations coming from this star were very important in the evolution of the first forms of life on Earth.

According to them, the star emits some pulses that has a huge influence on the pineal gland opening and equally its activation. The pine gland performs the function of assisting the body in orienting in space. It acts as a navigational centre. Asides from assisting the body in its space orientation, the pineal gland is also sensitive to magnetic field. One should also note that the pineal gland is sensitive to light and vibrations too. Some studies that was carried out on other animals with birds inclusive shows that the pineal gland monitors magnetic field. With the knowledge of the pineal gland acting as a navigational centre, it is easy to understand the role it plays in melatonin secretion which is laden with the responsibility of circadian rhythm. Circadian rhythms and melatonin secretion have a strong link to the receptivity to magnetic fields. It is therefore safe to say that stress on the physical body and geomagnetic storms can affect the pineal gland.

THE OPENING OF THE THIRD EYE STARTS WHEN THE PINEAL GLAND AND THE HEART VIBE IN SYNC

Because the pineal gland is sensitive to electromagnetic fields, the pineal gland in turn also responds to the heart's field which cause it to decalcify. A magnetic field is generated by the heart. The high and low vibration affects the entire body. The expansion of the of the electromagnetic field that is generated by the heart is amplified when we experience compassion, love and joy. So when the third eye only starts to open when the pineal gland and the heart have been synchronized, thus helping us to develop inner vision capacity, inspiration and intuition.

In conclusion, awakening your third eye gives you a sense of fulfilment as you are more in sync with the earth's magnetic force. Its rhythm and vibration soothes you. Have you ever tried to get a thought out of your head but it seems difficult? The more you engage your body in the exercises that helps activate your pineal gland, you find that you are more at peace. Difficult thoughts can now be placed aside. You can now choose to experience inner silence because stressful thoughts have been cast away.

Remember, sunbathe and sun gaze without sun shades and sun screen. Walk barefoot to stimulate the glands in your body. This helps in the activation of your third eye.

The more you awaken your third eye; you are expanding your consciousness. We possess multiple types of receptors that aid in interpreting and processing the messages we get from the sun though the message or information we get from the sun is constant. The most effective way to get used to the information the sun sends us is to sunbathe and sun gaze as earlier stated. Take time out to get a minimum 3o minutes exposure to sun, daily, without applying or using any sunscreen. This procedure will help you synthetize natural vitamin D.

CHAPTER 9: ACTIVATION OF HIGHER CONSCIOUSNESS

Human beings are naturally engineered to be aware of nature but there is a higher level to everything including a state of consciousness. Higher consciousness, as the term implies, is a transcended form of awareness that incurs deeper understanding of reality and spiritual development. Higher consciousness makes vague analysis of one's life become clear. It also clears whatever barrier could be hindering a person and self-improvement. You need to understand that life does not just encompass random series of events that happen as a result of choices made. Instead, it is an intelligent unfolding that is revealing itself to you all day long, bringing you step-by-step from unconsciousness into a state of higher consciousness. Your life, then, becomes a journey from unconsciousness to higher consciousness. Everything is a part of this evolution, including you. You are life evolving from unconsciousness into higher consciousness. Your life is not a random series of events. Your life is a journey from unconsciousness to higher consciousness. Michael Beckwith, minister of the Agape Church, describes this evolution in four phases and added two more, "Life happens in you" and "Life happens for you," and called them the "Six Phases of Higher Consciousness."

THE FIRST LEVEL OF HIGHER CONSCIOUSNESS IS WHEN "LIFE HAPPENS TO YOU".

Naturally, we believe everything that happens bids to affect us in every way. From the bad to the good, from the beautiful to the ugly, we believe they all happen to us as life unfolds and because we have little or no idea of what will happen next, we decide to let life take control and we ,thereby, become victims. In this level, you tend to be more open with and to life and you take everything life offers as it is. Since, you cannot control the happenings around you. So, you do not seem like much of a victim, you try to put two and two together and figure out why life is happening to you. This makes you imbibe the spirit of acceptance.

This takes me to the second level of Higher Consciousness, which is when:

No one really likes to be controlled or bossed around. Therefore, we would naturally see life as a threat and try to put it under our control. We start to plan and scheme and hope that our plans fall into place regardless of what life has in store for us. This makes us have a sense of responsibility over our lives. In this phase of consciousness, you make goals and create intentions, hopefully things will turn out as planned and you may play mockery of life. Also, you may eventually get what you want if you are loyal and committed to the goals. Control can also stem from having the right thoughts about your goals and mentally visualising your reality. When you have lived this level of consciousness long enough, you see the downside of it. First, you find yourself becoming fearful of your thoughts, believing that you should not be thinking that way because you would want to manifest your goals in your world. Second, it can also bring forth shame, for when it doesn't work the way you wished it should, you think this is because you haven't done it right enough or well enough.

After believing that life happens to you, you later tend to move to the third level of Higher Consciousness, which is when:

"LIFE HAPPENS IN YOU"

In this phase, you would have realised that being in control does not pay off after all. You don't attain the joy you really wanted. So, instead of being the victim or being the boss, you decide that maybe life needs to be opened to. At this level of consciousness, you begin to realize something very interesting: most of the time, rather than experiencing Life, you think about it, seeing only the thoughts in your head. When you experience Life through your thoughts, you stop experiencing it as it is. Or, as the well-known French author Anais Nin once said, "We don't see things as they are. We see them as we are."

It is in this phase of higher consciousness that you also realize that your suffering doesn't come from the experiences of your life. Instead it comes from your stories about what is happening. It comes from inside of you! There could be a good day and you're just fine. Then on another good day you could be miserable. You may either blame it on the day or the story behind the day. This is where you begin to live what we have been calling the you-turn. You become less interested in being a victim to your life or even trying to make it be any different than it is. You realize that the healing you long for comes when you turn your attention within. When you get to know the spells that are the source of your suffering, you can unhook from them and come back to Life. Gradually, you are activating your higher consciousness.

The next level of Higher Consciousness is:

"LIFE HAPPENS FOR YOU"

This is the phase in which you take note of what is happening to you and you turn it into pieces that make you a whole. The series of events are knotted together to make sense of your life so you would believe each day is a step closer into your full recognition, So, instead of falling victim under life or trying to control life, you relax and take note of these events as they unfold your true self and you are one step further on the journey to higher consciousness.

Life is not a random series of events. It is a highly intelligent unfolding that is putting you in the exact situations you need in order to see and unhook from the spells that keep you separate from its flow. No matter what is happening in your life, you finally understand that Life knows what it is doing. At this level of consciousness, rather than Life being something, you have to mold and shape into what you want it to be, you begin to show up for Life exactly as it is. Yes, the flow of Life includes pain, loss and death. But resisting the pains of Life only turn them it into suffering, and the suffering that comes from resistance is always much greater than directly experiencing your pain. Instead of tightening around your experiences and turning away from them, which only thickens your cloud bank of struggle, you bring your attention to your experience, whatever it is.

Remember: "Life is not a random series of events. It is a highly intelligent unfolding."

228

Even little moments of curiosity about what is going on right now sprinkled throughout your day are powerful! Every time you respond rather than react to what is going on inside of you, what was formerly bound up begins to loosen. Remember, your natural state is free-flowing aliveness. When that aliveness gets trapped in the spells, your energy and joy dim. When the spells receive the light of your attentiveness, they let go, and the trapped energy flows freely, bringing with it the bliss of openness.

The fifth level of Higher Consciousness is that:

"LIFE HAPPENS THROUGH YOU"

While the fourth phase of higher consciousness shows you that there is no such thing as an ordinary or basic moment in your life, in this phase, you will discover that Life is speaking to you at all moments and you would begin to take note of every moment. Becoming curious about what you are experiencing and giving it the light of compassionate attention so it can let go, you evolve into the next level of consciousness of allowing Life to move through you. This is where you recognize that Life is trustable. It is not always likable, but it knows what it is doing. Imagine a life where you trust Life implicitly.

Every morning you wake up with a sense of discovery and learning with your curious mind and your receptive heart. Rather than struggling with Life, you open to it, even when you are facing deep challenges. If you find yourself caught in reaction, you give your reaction the attention it needs to let go. Just then would you feel the vibrant flow of energy that Life can now move freely through you and this brings forth the joy and aliveness you so deeply long for. Creativity that you could never imagine on your own becomes clear to you, blessing yourself and everyone you meet with the wisdom of the meadow of Life.

You experience deep appreciation and gladness for absolutely everything. You see that your life is dependent on every ounce of creativity that has ever happened in the universe. You also see that all that has happened to you, even the difficult, has been a part of your journey back into Life. Step by step Life is bringing you into higher consciousness, into the ability to be fully here for Life. Now you can relax and show up for the adventure.

As Cynthia Bourgeault so beautifully says in her book Mystical Hope, "You find your way by being sensitively and sensually connected to exactly where you are, letting 'here' reach out and lead you."

The sixth Level of Higher Consciousness is:

"LIFE IS YOU"

It will get to a stage whereby you see life as your other half. You mirror life and life mirrors you. You creatively flow in and out of life with zero fear or doubt. So instead of trying to control life or reacting to life, you become more in sync with life and you discover that life is YOU. You realise that you are not merely a part of life but life in itself. As Eckhart Tolle said, "You are not in the universe; you are the universe, an intrinsic part of it. Ultimately you are not a person, but a focal point where the universe is becoming conscious of itself. What an amazing miracle. "The more you discover this, the more you are able to understand everything that happens in your life and the significance of these things.

As you analyse the Six Phases of Higher Consciousness, you will realise that the first two are about fixing, changing, resisting and trying to control Life. These phases are the world of your storyteller that doesn't know how to open to Life and believes he can have what he wants if he just thinks right. Throughout both of these levels of consciousness, there is a veil between you and the living experience of Life because neither phase is about showing up for the creative river of Life.

The next two phases of higher consciousness are about using your mind to be curious about what is happening rather than resisting and controlling. In Life is happening in you, you recognize that the storyteller inside of you is what separates you from Life. So rather than trying to change anything, you become interested in what you are experiencing in any given moment. The more you are here for Life, the easy and the difficult, the joyous and the sorrowful, unhooking from all of your spells, the clearer it becomes that Life knows what it is doing, and it is for you.

The final two phases of higher consciousness are all about coming home to the meadow. The more you live the truth that Life is for you, the more you relax into the flow, bringing you to the joy of Life moving through you. As your cloud bank dissipates, you not only recognize the meadow again, you recognize that you are the meadow! Life is you and you are Life!

Most people live in the first two phases of higher consciousness, to you and by you, never knowing that right in the middle of these beliefs is a doorway into the last four. Life is waking you up from the contraction of the first two and into the opening of the last four. This is not only for your own healing, but for the healing of all beings, because as you see through your cloud bank of struggle, you become a healing presence in the world.

The truth is that these phases make up our lives, none is dispensable. If you really want to activate higher consciousness, they are phases to undergo. Human beings are evolving from the first level of consciousness to the sixth. It is also true that most days you will experience a number of these phases. It is not about getting rid of any particular phase or making one better than the other. They are all part of Life, and as you evolve, you will recognize and be able to embrace them all.

As you activate higher levels of consciousness, you become less concerned in trying to change anything in your life and more interested in what is going on inside of you, especially in difficult situations. You have a deeper sense of granting life the permission to put you in the exact situations you need in order for the core spells that make up your reality to be brought to the surface of your awareness. It is there that you can see them, watch them in action, and discover that they are just spells that were conditioned into you when you were young and that you no longer need to wallow in them.

It is almost as if these sensitive spells of fear, shame, doubt, jealousy, low self-esteem, loneliness, and anger, to name a few, are like butterflies that have been trapped inside of you. But rather than the feeling being good, it is inkling. As your resistance to experiencing them lessens, they begin to loosen, arising to the surface to be seen. As they are fully seen, they burst, and the energy that was formerly trapped in them lets go. Rather than being afraid of this purification process, you begin to welcome it as the longing to be fully awake to Life becomes stronger than the fear of your spells. Pause for a moment and take a deep breath. Allow any holding you discover there to melt away and let a smile fill you with its healing presence. Allow this softening to move all the way down to your sole. Feel the essence of your unfolding higher consciousness.

Even in a difficult situation, you are able to figure things out and instead of hitting the rock bottom, you bounce right back and move forward. So, rather than become victim under life and dwell in the vagueness of your life's reality, you should come alive to higher consciousness and drive the car of your life with life itself at the passenger's seat. You will need to trust life. When you do, life would not just happen through you but you will be able to control how it does. You will be able to hold things you want to hold and let go the ones you want to let go of.

Even feelings like aloneness, or unending sadness, or the black hole of nothingness that seem so deep and real when you are resisting them become something to say "hello" to and touch with compassion. As you stand with them, they no longer have the power over you they used to have, and the energy that was bound up in them is released, opening you to the meadow that is always with you. As often as you activate higher consciousness, you would realise that that peace, comfort and joy you have always wanted to have always been part of you. You may not notice it at the spur of the moment just yet but when you are more open to life and you let life happen through you, you would recognise and live from the meadow of your being.

Learning how to meditate can help you to achieve higher consciousness faster, because when your mind is clear and focused, and your body is relaxed and calm, you can access information, both internal and external, that can help you make better decisions.

The more you meditate, the more access you have to your intuition which would in turn transcend you into higher consciousness. Meditation is a practice where you train your mind or induce a state of consciousness. You can meditate to realize some benefit, such as relaxation, stress reduction, healing, or strengthening your life force. Or for developing certain qualities such as love, patience, generosity, and forgiveness.

Focusing on breathing, visualizations, mantras or meditation music can help bring mindfulness to the present moment. This sets the stage to calm your mind.

Most importantly, meditation can also be used to access inner wisdom and insight from your own higher unconscious or from a Universal power often referred to as God, infinite Intelligence, Universal Consciousness, or Source.

For most people, the basic way to meditate is to close the eyes, slow down breathing, focus goals by repeating a phrase without being distracted by anything else. Whereas some people have a resistance to meditation. They think it's too weird at first. Or they say they're too busy to take the time to learn how to meditate. Moreover, there are many different forms of meditation that have been developed over thousands of years in many diverse cultures. But the reality is that you're focusing on one thing so that everything else begins to drop away. During meditation, your mind quiets. You're able to access your subconscious mind. When you first start meditating, you may notice that your mind begins to wander.

If you sit with your eyes closed, trying not to think a thought, you'll probably end up pretty frustrated, because your mind will tend to wander and you'll think you're failing, which is fine. It's much easier when you have guidance, when there's meditation music, when someone's voice is guiding you through the steps. Your mind doesn't wander as much, and it's much easier to follow along and not get lost in all the stories and the to-do lists and the thinking about the past and worrying about the future that we normally do.

CONCLUSION

I believe before you got your hand on this book, you are either a psychic or you have a friend that is a psychic who wants to know more and develop has psychic abilities. Very possible fact is, you do not fall in any of the category, but you are just curious about who a psychic is or if they were real. In all you are welcome because i want to believe that this book sorted out your needs.

Hope you had a great time enlightening yourself from this guide?

Your third eye goes beyond the natural. Of course, you only have two eyes in the natural. Your third eye is your mind eyes, the eyes of your soul. Its very possible to actually see things without the natural eyes. You get to see beyond the boundaries of the natural world. Many people do not know of how much value it is to put your third eyes to use. Your mind eyes! There is so much meditation can do for you. It is true when there say much meditation brings about maturity. You engage your mind on something you either knew and then it broadens your mind into thoughts that becomes real to you.

Other times meditation can be in a way you can actually shut activities in your mind and make your physical senses to become really sensitive and very active. Meditation connects your soul to your body. Just like yoga. Meditation goes a long way and with the different kinds of meditation, you should deliberately put it to practice.

NOW TALKING ABOUT BEING A PSYCHIC IN PROPER.

You probably didn't know that your psychic abilities can be improved upon. But you just did with much meditation, patience, believing in yourself, maintaining a positive attitude, being creative, deliberately communing with your soul and of course continuous practice.

KEEP PRACTICING!

It's like flexing your muscles and in no time, you are in control. Things doesn't just happen without you knowing because you have mastered how to use them. Being a psychic is being gifted. So now you can use your gifts at will. Learning about the different abilities should help you know how to recognise, focus and channel each abilities. Like I had earlier said, before you know how to use your intuition. People say, "what you don't know cannot work for you". In essence, you must be able to recognise it. Until you are able to recognise it, you cannot use what you don't have and now that you know that you have intuition, the wise thing to do would be to make use of it.

There are times in life when you can find anyone to rely on all you'd have is your instincts. You need to learn to trust in your instincts. Your intuition is a powerful force that you must use to your advantage. So, you must master using it. Always work on it when you get one and in so doing you can actually use it to your advantage. Learn how to open your heart and mind to what you are capable of. Only then will your intuition be your guiding light on your journey through life.

Again, meditation helps your intuition to be sharper. Because in meditation you tend to give room for your soul to commune with you and your senses are sharper to receive what is being said to you. This is very common with introverts but, whether you are an introvert or an extrovert you can actually consciously put this into practice. Try following this guide and you would see it works.

Talking about the spiritual aspect and how to develop your psychic ability. The Pineal Gland, the hypothalamus and the pituitary have significant roles to play in the activation and awakening process the spiritual development.

 The limbic system which is the centre if our emotions and feelings is connected to the hypothalamus. We have learnt that the hypothalamus and the pituitary gland are involved in regulating all of our basic survival needs, from food, which is hunger to thirst, our sleep and even our growth. The pineal gland is as important as being a psychic itself

Being a psychic is being gifted. For you to be a psychic, you have to see it as being blessed. You are not weird. Whatever is happening to you is something many would need. So, you have to believe in yourself, stay positive always.

You decide how to make use of your gifts. You can use your gifts to touch lives, help people, help yourself.

CPSIA information can be obtained
at www.ICGtesting.com
Printed in the USA
BVHW050259300921
617791BV00014BA/344